SOUTHSIDE VIRGINIA
Chronicles

JOHN CAKNIPE JR.

Charleston London

THE
History
PRESS

Published by The History Press
Charleston, SC 29403
www.historypress.net

Copyright © 2014 by John Caknipe Jr.
All rights reserved

First published 2014

Manufactured in the United States

ISBN 978.1.62619.503.5

Library of Congress CIP data applied for.

CONTENTS

CONTENTS

Acknowledgements

Thanks to Womack Publishing Company, Inc., for printing many of my stories in the series: "Remember the Gray" in the *South Hill Enterprise*, South Hill, Virginia, and "Unsung Heroes" in the *News Progress*, Chase City, Virginia, since the spring of 2009. Thank you to editors Nick Elmes, who, while the editor of the *News Progress*, encouraged me to write the stories and then encouraged my writing a second series when he went to the *Enterprise*; Jeff Humber, editor of the *News Progress* in 2009 and 2010, for his support and encouragement in publishing my first series of stories; and Dallas Weston for continuing to publish the stories as space became available. Also, thank you to Patrick Love, managing editor of Womack Publishing for the *Enterprise*, for his blessing for this project. Thank you to the late Sarah Bearas, editor at the Virginia Historical Society, Library of Virginia, for her support of my stories and inclusion in the Virginia Biography Series.

Since the stories were published, I have completed more research and spoken with a lot more descendants of families from the region. I have completed the reading of the Board of Supervisors Records from 1870 to 1951 and circuit court record books for 1830 through 1871. The stories previously published have been updated with the additional findings, and new stories, which never made it to print, have been added for this volume.

A big thank-you goes to Mark Pace, research librarian/historian, for stories, photos, research, support and use of resources of the Richard H. Thornton Library, Granville County Library System, Oxford, North Carolina. Thank you to Wanda Brooks, historian, Southside Regional

Library, Boydton, Virginia, for her assistance and support. Thank you to my wife, Betty McKinney Caknipe, for taking many of the photographs, scanning and all the driving excursions. I'd also like to thank her for her patience in putting up with my new passion for the history of the region.

I sincerely want to thank the citizens of the Piedmont area for their support with stories, family histories and photos, as well as purchases of the newspapers to follow my stories and purchases of previous books on the Southside history. Finally, I wish to thank Beth Coates, director, and the staff and volunteers of the South Boston–Halifax County Museum of History and Art for their gracious assistance with research and resources. Their genealogy center is staffed by several friendly and supportive volunteer historians.

INTRODUCTION

Little was known about the Piedmont region in the seventeenth century, except that the governor of Virginia wanted to establish a relationship with the Indians for trade. He offered incentives for adventurers to explore and settle in the Wild West, build a ferry system to cross the rivers and establish trading posts. The goal was to enhance the fur trading with the Sapony Nation, especially the Occoneechee tribe, which had established a reputation as the trade Mecca on the East Coast for fifteen nations ranging from Syracuse, New York, to Savannah, Georgia. But then in 1678, the famous Nathaniel Bacon raid and brutal attack on the Occoneechee tribe on Occoneechee Island and at Fort Occoneechee changed the mission and signaled that the Wild West was no longer wild. In the early 1700s, a treaty was signed by the governor of the colony of Virginia with some bands of Indians. It was referred to as the Treaty of the Middle Plantation and included the lands south of the Appomattox and Blackwater Rivers. This provided for a protected area for the Indians south of the rivers and a protected area for the new settlers north of the rivers.

Then, in 1705, the House of Burgesses decided to amend the boundaries. The new protected area, for the Indians, was an area six miles in circumference, near the southwest border of Brunswick County. This opened the Southside Virginia area to development and exploration but resulted in the Tuscarora Indians along the south side of the Roanoke River in North Carolina staging a violent revolt. The new governor of Virginia, Alexander Spotswood, believed that a community with a trading post, fort and nearby Indian community could bolster westward migration by quelling some of the violence. Thus, he sought to enhance trade routes and increase income, trade and taxes. In 1714, Fort Christanna in Brunswick County, Virginia, was built.

In 1733, Colonel William Byrd arrived in the region to survey a boundary line between North Carolina and Virginia. The new boundary included a strip south of the river. In some cases, this divided old Royal Land Grants, patents and warrants, with lands being located in both states. The Piedmont region became primarily the counties of Brunswick, Mecklenburg, Charlotte, Lunenburg, Halifax and Pittsylvania in Virginia and Granville, Vance, Warren, Person and Halifax in North Carolina. Some of the early settlers to the region were prominent in U.S. history, such as Randolph, Hopkins, Lee, Marshall and Jefferson. The rivers that needed numerous ferry crossings and settlements in Virginia were the Roanoke, Dan, Hyco, Bannister and Meherrin.

West of Occoneechee, Byrd noted a mineral spring. He also wrote that his guides shot a buffalo standing in a creek for food and dubbed the waterway Buffalo Creek. This area became Buffalo Mineral Springs resort, dating to circa 1789, and was visited by Thomas Jefferson and many other notables. The resort encompassed over 120 acres of land, plus several adjacent farms for support near the intersection of the Hyco and Dan Rivers. With a development of several springs, a water bottling company, multiple hotels, cottages, sporting event areas and supporting buildings, the resort remained operational until 1940. It served as a respite for many during the Civil War. The resort featured entertainers from Virginia and North Carolina, and at one point in 1920–21, it employed the Epson family (Buddy Epson, along with his sister and father). There were other mineral springs in Southside, including Ogburn's in Flat Creek, Palmer Springs Resort, Mecklenburg Mineral Springs in Chase City and others.

In 1798, General Samuel Hopkins (brother of Johns Hopkins), from Palmer Springs, Mecklenburg County, Virginia, and Granville County, North Carolina, was offered the position of surveyor for the western territory of Kentucky, and he accepted. Several prominent families from the Piedmont region followed him west. Some went to Tennessee and Arkansas, while others traveled to Alabama, Mississippi and Kentucky. Many took their pedigree horses with them. One family of note was John and Mary G. Poor James. John was the grandson of notable William James from England. Arriving in Kentucky from the Dan River area of Pittsylvania County, Virginia, one of John and Mary's sons was Reverend Richard James, a Baptist preacher.

He then moved to Missouri in 1842 to establish a church and became the founder of a Baptist college. His youngest son, Jesse Woodson James, was born there, in 1847.

The Piedmont Region claims several major historical accomplishments. The first is that it was referenced in the late eighteenth and early nineteenth centuries as the "Old Race Horse Region." In 1811, the area horses were the focus in Greenville County, Virginia, but most of the gentry planters from the Piedmont owned and bred many Thoroughbreds, and Southside became noted for the introduction of a new breed: quarter horses. The area has been referred to as the "Cradle of Methodism" in the United States, hosting one of the first Methodist academies—Ebenezer, circa 1784—and the first successful continuous Methodist college in the United States, Randolph Macon College (1830) in Boydton, Virginia.

In decades past, the Piedmont had been a flood plain, with flooding occurring about every seven to ten years. In the 1920s, the U.S. Army Corps of Engineers began surveying and researching the area to create a dam and lake system. This was begun in the 1940s and completed in the 1960s. The system ranged from near Bedford, Virginia, to Rocky Mount, North Carolina. During the excavating of the rivers in preparation for the dams, evidence of Native American communities and workshops was found that dated back over fifteen thousand years, but most interesting were the specimens of iron tools and medallions found in the Halifax County region that dated to the sixteenth century. The artifacts could have been from the Spanish explorers who came west, following the James River, in 1566 or from their second trip in 1570.

In April 1865, when the Civil War was nearing its end, Richmond was evacuated. The train, carrying the president, cabinet and Confederate treasury traveled through Southside, stopping in Danville. President Davis stayed at the Sutherlin mansion in Danville, and it has become known as the last capital of the Confederacy. Several sources have speculated that the gold shipment, at the close of the war, mysteriously disappeared between Richmond and Georgia. The mansion survives and is the present-day Sutherlin Mansion–Danville Museum of History and Fine Arts.

ANTEBELLUM

Gold, Silver, Copper and Tungsten Mining in the Piedmont

When William Byrd II (1674–1744) was commissioned to survey the border between Virginia and North Carolina, he found a vast wilderness of Indians, streams and wild game, including elk and buffalo. He wrote an interesting notation in his journal of 1729 that within two miles of the Hyco River mouth, there were good "shows of copper mines." He wrote about the ornamental jewelry of the local Indians and the wildlife. So impressed with the area was he that he proclaimed the area of Southside Virginia as "the garden from which Adam drank," and he patented over 100,000 acres for his own use in southern Virginia and purchased over 20,000 acres of what became Granville County, North Carolina. Once a patent was claimed and registered, the owner had to demonstrate that he was using the property. Byrd hired several British and colonial militia as overseers to come to the area and establish a residence in his name and to begin clearing and tilling the land. One such overseer built a home for Byrd on the Stanton (aka Roanoke) River at the mouth of the big Bluestone Creek.

Another individual who was notable in the area was Colonel Drury Stith, surveyor for Brunswick County in 1730. In the latter 1730s, when Byrd and Stith came through the area to check on their properties, they discovered a haggard-looking man, who stated that he had not had meat in two weeks, and he was working the Stith copper mine on the bank of Allen's Creek. He was living in a dilapidated lean-to. (There were numerous mines, operated early on by the Native American Indians, on the Hyco and Dan Rivers before 1700, as referenced by Byrd.) Mines were also being worked on the banks of Butcher's Creek and Bluestone Creek, where Byrd had "Bluestone Castle" built. The Stith family then moved and settled on Allen's Creek in about 1750, east of present day Boydton, Virginia.

About 1840, one mile north on Allen's Creek (the longest creek in the county and very close to meeting the designation of river), John B. Tunstall began operation of his gold/silver mine. In 1850, the mine area became a gristmill and sawmill operation. Following the example of the former Indian inhabitants, new settlers were mining gold, silver and copper along the banks of most of the designated creeks and rivers in Mecklenburg, Pittsylvania, Halifax and Charlotte Counties in Virginia, as well as in Person, Vance and Granville Counties of North Carolina. Much of this was referred to as the Virgilina Vein.

Most of the early mine records list that they were being worked by a mining overseer, generally with his family, and two or three slaves. Most of the tunnels were "head deep." John Butcher, for whom Butcher's Creek is named, owned several hundred acres around 1730 in present-day Chase City. One story written about him dates to about 1733: "Mr. Butcher received us kindly. This honest man set a mighty value on the mine he fancied he had in his pasture and showed us some of the ore, which he was made to believe was a gray copper and would certainly make his fortune."

In 1890, a 120-acre parcel of the northeastern section of John Butcher's farm in Burwell's Quarters (Fairview) was sold to an investor, who began mining kaolin until the mine was closed in 1920. A second kaolin deposit was discovered in the 1890s, and another mine was established. The mine was located on a 220-acre parcel of land southwest of Scotts Crossroads and old Concord Road intersection. The Mecklenburg County Deed Book lists the farm and mine as being purchased in 1919 by Adelia A. Saunders. The mine closed in 1920 and never reopened.

"Everywhere there are mines," Byrd wrote around 1740. "I am sorry to say it, but idleness is the general character of the men in the southern parts of this colony as well as in North Carolina." A minimum of work was necessary due to the climate and the abundance of resources. "There was plenty of promise beneath the ground too. Since the days of the Roanoke Colony, [there have been] rumors of the existence of copper...and [many have] found the rumors to be true...The people are all mine-mad...Mr. Stith was the first that was seized with the frenzy."

But with the California gold rush in the late 1840s, most all the claims and mines in this locale were abandoned until the late 1880s. With the coming of the railroad to the area, there was a renewed interest in mining

Map of the Virgilina Gold Vein with listing of abandoned mines and prospects. The vein extends into North Carolina. *Courtesy of Virginia Division of Mineral Resources.*

the Piedmont Region. The mining and mineralogy maps referred to the area as the Virgilina Gold Vein. The Virgilina district is well defined as beginning on the southwest fringe of the area five miles southwest of Virgilina at the border of Person and Granville Counties, North Carolina, at the Duke Mine, with a lot of quartz veins containing copper. This is near Cedar Grove Church and Allenville, at Cressent Mine, and near Durgy Mine and Copper World Mine. To the east are Ford Prospect, near Royster School in Granville County, and Gillis Mine, near Olive Branch Church. Next are Eagle Prospects and Durgy Gold Prospects, on Crooked Creek, and then north to King Copper mine and a cluster of about twenty mines and prospects in Halifax County, Virginia. In Granville County, one of the longest-operating and most profitable mines was the Blue Wing Mine. Next was the Holloway Prospects and Holloway Mine, which is located three miles south and one mile east of Virgilina. From this mine, approximately 180,000 tons of ore were taken during the operating years. According to Reverend Harry Mathis in his 1964 book, *Along the Border*, "It was considered one of the most promising prospects in the Virgilina District."

PIEDMONT PLATEAU, BURWELL'S QUARTERS AND AN EARLY GENTRY PLANTER

One of the most influential people in the Piedmont was Colonel Lewis Burwell. The original Burwell descendants came to the New World as first settlers, having originated from Bedford in Northhampton, England. Edward Burwell arrived in Virginia in 1607 with a land grant from King James. The land grant was for Burwell Bay and Isle of Wright County, Virginia Colony. His son Major Lewis Burwell married Lucy, daughter of Captain Higginson, in 1658. After the marriage, Lewis and his brother Nathaniel moved to King William County.

Lewis Burwell was born in Williamsburg, Virginia, along with seven brothers and sisters. His grandfather, also named Lewis, was president of the Virginia Colony when the younger Lewis visited the Piedmont in 1751. Because of the discovery of the rich curative mineral waters of the area, he patented 4,300 acres of land along a ridge, which was later surveyed and titled the Piedmont Plateau. But before Lewis could develop the land, he died in 1756. One of his reasons for visiting the area was to inspect the grant given to his son, Armistead. Armistead had married Christian Blair and received a dower land grant from King George IV. The grant was for 3,404 acres on Finneywood branch, issued in 1746, but Armistead never came to the region.

Instead, in 1768, when Armistead's son Lewis married Ann Spotswood, Lewis was given the land as a gift. Ann Spotswood was the granddaughter of Governor Alexander Spotswood. Spotswood was a member of the renowned "Knights of the Golden Horseshoe" and was said to have been the wisest governor of Virginia. As a wedding gift, they were given a grant of 2,500 acres, which bordered the land of his grandfather that he had inherited. Living in Gloucester, Lewis Burwell was a true gentleman of the racetrack and Thoroughbred racehorses. On May 5, 1768, his horse, Remus, was entered in four races. Each race had a purse of one hundred pounds (a huge sum in those days) that drew extremely large bets on the side—as much as ten thousand pounds of tobacco on one race for one bet. Many fortunes were made and lost at the racetracks in those days.

In 1775, Lewis was serving as a naval officer at the ports of the James River. In 1781, Governor Thomas Jefferson appointed Lewis lieutenant of the recently organized (1765) Mecklenburg County. That year, along with his brother, Thacker, Lewis and his family moved to the Piedmont Plateau. They built Stoneland, said to be the largest home in the region, with twenty rooms, and they developed Mecklenburg County's first community, Burwell's Quarters.

In 1746, Lunenburg County was formed from Brunswick County, which was huge, spreading from Southside Virginia west to include present-day southeastern West Virginia, eastern Kentucky and a section of the southern Ohio River Valley. For each region, a court was needed, and one of the first was in Southside. A courthouse had to be centrally located in the community served, so by latitude and longitude, the spot was determined, for the area needing surveyed. That spot was in the northwest quadrant of Armistead Burwell's land grant.

When the surveyors and courthouse committee arrived, they camped on the southern edge of what they labeled the Piedmont Plateau (sometimes referred to as the dividing ridge) at Burwell's Quadrant. The ridge serves as a natural watershed for the area that directs all water north of the plateau to the Meherrin River and all water south of the plateau to the Roanoke River. Some immediately protested the lack of water access, so the committee began to scout the area and discovered the headwater of what became Little Bluestone Creek. Approximately one mile southwest along the creek, they found a high, level area with open fields and sparse vegetation, suitable for a courthouse. When they returned with their findings and recommendations, Burwell's Quadrant became known as Burwell's Quarters, and around 1890, it became known as Fairview.

John Murray, of Scotland, and his wife, Ann Bolling, offered to build the courthouse, stocks, public pillory and a house for officials to use. Colonel Lewis Delony offered to build a prison and clerk's office, with a cabinet for books and records and a table for the court clerk. There were many protests over the location of the courthouse, but it was built according to the committee's specifications in 1746. In 1765, Mecklenburg County and Charlotte County were carved from part of Lunenburg County. The Lunenburg County court had to be relocated, and Mecklenburg County had to build a courthouse in a more accessible location. The prison was never built.

Before the community was completed, Ann Burwell died in 1782, following the birth of their twelfth child—Elizabeth. Later, when the community was completed, it was composed of a cooperage, butcher shop, two smokehouses, two meat storage houses, a tanning yard, blacksmith shops, a large icehouse and stables. On the Meherrin River was a large gristmill and grain store house. There was a practice track for Burwell's racehorses, along with a community store and additional stables for visitors.

The famous Shadow of Janus pedigree stood stud from 1781 to 1783 at Burwell's Quarters. Burwell had already owned Remus, and from his stand, he acquired Phoenix from the pedigree of Shadow, Janus, Jolly Roger and Regulus. The latter became a very valuable horse.

During the Revolutionary War, Burwell was the county lieutenant, in command of the militia. He was then directed to take charge of militias from the counties of Brunswick, Lunenburg and Mecklenburg. He was promoted to colonel. For his outstanding service, he received a warrant for 2,500 acres of land in Mecklenburg County. In 1786, he was elected to the newly established Virginia House of Delegates, where he served, representing Southside, until his death in 1800. At his death, he was considered Mecklenburg County's wealthiest man.

While serving in the House of Delegates, Burwell met and married Elizabeth Harrison in 1789. She was a close cousin of the future president of the United States. As a wedding gift, they received a patent for a 2,500-acre tract of land adjoining his father's grant on Finneywood Creek, which now included Black Branch. In the 1790s, Burwell was a very busy man. He was one of a handful of elite gentry planters of the region, operating two distinct, vast plantations totaling over 12,000 acres, and he, along with John Cunningham (who was married to Justice John Marshall's sister) and Samuel Puryear (who had married the daughter of Clausel Clausel), took over operation of the Christiansville racetrack (which was located next to the southwestern corner of his property on a 288-acre parcel of land that had been established as the Christiansville Tract, in the 1780s).

Lewis, Elizabeth and their children were members of the local Episcopal church, which had begun in 1766 and was located in the old courthouse building. In 1791, the couple had a new baby. They presented themselves to the church, along with their children and families of their children, friends and neighbors, to have the baby christened. For the failing little church following the war, this was a great revival.

Accompanying the elder Burwell were his sons: Colonel John Spotswood Burwell and family; Colonel Peyton R. Burwell and family; Captain Armistead Burwell with his wife, Mary; and Lewis's sister, Miss Jane Burwell. Also in attendance was Burwell's daughter, Ann Spotswood Burwell, with her husband, John S. Ravenscroft, who was a student at William and Mary College in Williamsburg, Virginia. When twenty-five new people arrive in a small church, there is an instant revival. At this revival, John Ravenscroft (referred to at college as "Mad Jack" because of his temper) received a conversion, returned to William and Mary and began to study theology.

Colonel Lewis Burwell and Elizabeth had four children. Of the children born to him and Ann, I have presented three sons and a daughter. There are only two others that I know of. The eldest, Mary Armistead Burwell, married Samuel Goode. Goode was the first United States congressman from Southside. The third daughter was Matilda. She married Alexander Boyd Jr., founder and developer of the new Mecklenburg Courthouse community, which became Boyd's Town and then, in 1812, was changed to Boydton. The youngest, Elizabeth, married Edward L. Tabb. As dower, they were given a parcel of three hundred acres on what became Barnesville Road (present-day Mecklenburg Electric Cooperative Corporate office). Edward Tabb died in April 1832, and the estate was to be administered by Samuel Goode, with John Ravenscroft & Company, Elizabeth's brothers-in-law.

Though Colonel Lewis Burwell died in 1800, it wasn't until 1803 that an inventory of his property was recorded. This was a seven-page inventory of personal property, excluding real estate. Most of his horses had been disposed of, as the inventory only listed a total of thirteen. The inventory also listed eighty-two slaves, but most interesting was the library, of great value with almost two hundred volumes. Most of the books were bound, English versions, with multiple series, regarding lords and royalty. There were several volumes relating to trades, such as cooperage, blacksmithing, farming and milling.

Following the death of Colonel Lewis Burwell, his son Captain Armistead became heavily involved in horse racing. In 1807, he purchased a stud, Post Boy, and that same year, he moved his family closer to the racing action to Waverly, Franklin County, Virginia. He was listed as a farmer and tobacco factor. In 1809, his son was born, John Spotswood Burwell (d. 1880). In the War of 1812, Armistead Burwell was promoted to the rank of colonel. In

Finch Parker feeding Thoroughbred Appaloosa stud Smokey Mountain Ghost in November 1962 on his farm in the Black Branch area. *Courtesy Tommy Parker.*

the 1820s, he sold some of his Southside holdings and moved his family to Dinwiddie County, just south of Petersburg. Horses are still a part of the Piedmont today.

The March 6, 1892 *Richmond Dispatch* has a lengthy article about the Burwell family, including Ravenscroft and the new Episcopal church. The Virginia Society for Historical Preservation had visited the "Stoneland Plantation" cemetery, which it found to be in ruins with one exception: the monument, which towers six feet high, three feet wide and several inches thick. The inscription was an acknowledgement of the Revolutionary War hero's family, listing his parents, wives and all the sixteen children with their spouses. The children include: Armistead, who married Lucy Crawley; Elizabeth, married to Edward Tabb; John, who married a woman with the

A monument in Burwell's Memorial Garden in the courtyard of the Chase City Episcopal Church, Fourth Street at Marshall. *Photo by Betty McKinney Caknipe.*

last name Woods; Christian, who married William Hamblin; Lewis, who married Sally Green; Panthea, married to Richard Boyd; Blair, married to Elizabeth Hatcher; Delia Harris Spotswood married Polly Marshall; Harriett, who died in infancy; H. Harrison, who married Catherine Buford; Peyton Randolph, who married Jane Sewell; Jean Blair, who married Colonel William Eaton (of Granville County, North Carolina); and Martha, who married Grandison Field and then John Field.

The monument was placed by J.S.R. Burwell and relatives sometime during the 1830s or 1840s. After the Virginia Historical Society's report that the cemetery was in shambles, the stone was removed from the abandoned cemetery to the front yard of the Chase City Episcopal Church. Sometime later, the congregation of the church built a garden memorializing it.

A GENTRY PLANTER'S LIBRARY

Pre–twentieth century, most children were home schooled or sent to school for limited studies that the family felt an instructor was better able to teach, and they started with the basics of reading and writing, primarily Greek and Latin. The subtle distinctions in the two languages aroused amusing anecdotes, poetry and use of imagination in critical thinking. Natural science, philosophy and mathematics would round out a good education. Schools gained popularity with an explosion of new academies and colleges in the 1820s and 1830s. Around 1850, at the advanced academies, natural science also included geology, physics and astrology. After 1860, in advanced studies, they added a course on English language and literature. But in the academy, English rounded out the trilogy of language requirements.

To put into perspective and describe an antebellum plantation home library, I chose Lewis Burwell's—primarily because it was the most legible. This should give an idea of the reading and study habits of the gentry, nobles and learned scholars (which included most teachers and preachers with educations). We can't omit women, as there were many who wanted to do more in life than just talk about babies, cooking and taking care of their men. During the morning sewing bee, held almost daily in the main house of most plantations, the mistress of the house or one of her children would often discuss with all in attendance a lesson for the day. In reading the list of the volumes contained in Lewis's library, note that most books on sermons were in Latin and others in Greek. Most all volumes in the collection were leather bound with Chinese paper and in limited quantity. No one book represented a lesson. For example, these volumes would offer some Spanish language, culture, morals and philosophies, geography and government.

(As a side note, on one of his visits to the area, I had an acquaintance read over the list of books. He was very impressed and knew most of the works. He is a retired professor of languages from Louisiana State University.)

- eight volumes: Humes, *History of England*
- ten volumes: Rolliers, *Ati History*
- eight volumes: "Spectator"
- six volumes: Pleitarch's *Lives*
- one volume: Euclid's *Elements*
- five volumes: "Precptor"
- one volume: Bayer's *Dictionary and Grammar*
- one volume: Buchan
- three volumes: Martaigne's *Essays*
- three volumes: History of California
- three volumes: Hawhesworth's *Voyages*
- six volumes: Paps Works
- one volume: Delaney's *Sermons*
- one volume: *A Young Man's Colt*
- four volumes: *Founding*
- two volumes: Fordye Sermons
- six volumes: Sermons
- two volumes: Conlan's *History*
- two volumes: Bishop Burnett's *History*
- one volume: *Massachusetts History*

At this juncture, the person taking the inventory decided to take a short cut. He wrote "91 volumes, Books, more." That ended the inventory. In the plantation homes, libraries contained sophisticated books for that time period. This was true of most of the successful antebellum homes. Standing in society not only was about being knowledgeable of current events but also required practical applications (common sense) and substance. Conversations were probably about history, geography, stars, philosophy, life and religion—much like today.

The library seemed to have served the desired purpose. Two of Burwell's sons became justices for the county, and all his children were educated, along with the daughters. Most of their children received an education with advanced studies. Several generations of Burwell sons went on to become doctors, teachers and lawyers. It was illegal to provide an education for slaves in Virginia after about 1805 (and especially after 1831) until after the Civil War, but the Burwells did anyway. In 1858, James Burwell, grandson of Colonel Lewis (who had inherited a sizable portion of Burwell's Quarters from his grandfather), freed his slaves, built a schoolhouse and hired a college-educated, free black teacher, Isaac Craighead, from Richmond. Craighead developed the boarding school for the freed slaves from Burwell's plantation and the freemen (and slaves, if they could attend) of the community. One of the first students from the neighborhood was Cephus Davis (b. 1843), a free man of color (one document lists "freed"), who lived on a farm nearby. (I have read the circuit court records of Mecklenburg County from 1830 through 1871, and no one was ever charged with the crime of teaching a slave, even though it was common knowledge that many did.)

Davis excelled in his studies and was accepted to Hampton Institute and then to Richmond Theological Institute, graduating in 1868. He returned to Christiansville and began preaching in several of the local Baptist churches from 1868 to 1876. During Reconstruction, blacks and whites were no longer allowed to attend church together. It was a federal mandate under martial law that they segregate. Many new churches and schools sprang up in the area. In 1876, Davis announced that he was retiring from the ministry to

The Fairview Tavern, later a juke joint, was razed in 2009. It was one of the last buildings of the Fairview community in Chase City. *Courtesy William C. Gregory.*

teach at the newly established Thyne Institute (Elementary School) for freed blacks, operated by the Presbyterian Mission Board of Pennsylvania. The school was located near Craighead's old schoolhouse in Burwell's Quarters, but with the opening of Thyne, the name of the neighborhood was changed to Fairview.

In the 1890s, with the popularity of mining operations in the county returning, many of the managers and executives arrived, accompanied by their servants. Travel was still slow by train and horse. To accommodate the servants, who were not allowed to stay in the hotels nor use the facilities, several boardinghouses opened for just that purpose. In 1906, one of Davis's cousins, along with some other black investors, purchased a seventeen-acre parcel of land near Thyne Institute and began preparation for the development of the Fairview Country Club. Nearby, another Davis cousin began a restaurant, Fairview Tavern, which, in the 1920s became a juke joint for citizens of the community (and students from the high school).

Alas, the Mecklenburg Hotel/Sanitarium burned in 1909, and the mines began to close that same year. The Fairview Country Club never materialized.

THOSE BURWELL WOMEN AND EDUCATION

During the War of 1812, the Burwell men distinguished themselves repeatedly. But on New Year's Eve 1815, tragedy struck the Burwell family. A letter from a neighbor, Mrs. E.B. Kennon, to the godmother of young Martha Burwell (Miss Rachael Morecai of Granville County, North Carolina) relates that Elizabeth Burwell's son Henry, with his wife and child; a grandson, Randolph, with his wife and the son-in-law; and John Burwell were sleeping at home (Stoneland). In addition, there were four black girls, and they were also sleeping upstairs. A fire had started in the kitchen and spread quickly. The letter stated, "The devouring flames blazed so violently that escape by the stairs was nearly impossible." But no lives were lost. As a matter of fact, most of the family escaped down the stairs, but one of the black girls was caught behind the blaze, and it was spreading quickly up the stairs. Henry went to the back of the house, called the girl and caught her as she jumped from the upstairs window.

In 1817, Armistead had a relationship with one of his slaves, and a daughter was born in February 1818. She was named Elizabeth Hobbs (d. May 1907). Elizabeth began work at the age of four as a nursemaid for the newborn baby in the home. She was taught to read and write as though she was one of the family. At the age of fourteen, she was sent to live with Armistead's son, Reverend Robert Burwell, who had just married Margaret Ann (Mary Anna) Robertson, of Chesterfield County, Virginia.

Armistead's oldest daughter, Ann, married the Honorable Hugh Garland, and they operated the Boydton Academy for three years from 1831 to 1833.

Hugh also served, for a short time, as the first principal/professor of the Randolph Macon Preparatory Academy in Boydton (October 1832 through March 1833). The youngest daughter, Ann Powell Burwell, married Hugh's younger brother, Landon Garland, at Boydton in December 1831. Landon became a professor at Randolph Macon College in 1832 and the second president of the college in 1836. Both of the Burwell women were educated and taught classes in the Boydton Academy. In 1833, Armistead became licensed to practice law.

In 1837, Reverend Robert and Margaret Burwell relocated to the Hillsborough Presbyterian Church, in Hillsborough, North Carolina, and he was pastor. They were settled, with Elizabeth, into the church manse. One of the first expressed needs of the congregation was a school. So Robert and Margaret began Burwell's School (for young ladies), in the manse, in 1837. When Robert was replaced as the minister, he purchased two lots next door and built a small brick school, but the school was closed in 1857. The Burwells moved to Charlotte, North Carolina, and began a school there. Burwell's school became the progenitor of Queens University of Charlotte.

We must return to the rest of the story of Armistead's slave daughter, Elizabeth Hobbs. She continued working in Hillsborough at Burwell's Academy but seems to have developed a disposition (pregnancy) that resulted in her being returned to Virginia in 1843. She became the property of Hugh and Ann Garland. The Garlands had some difficult times financially in the mid-1840s, and Elizabeth had learned to be an excellent seamstress. Her work and the income from it helped keep the family afloat for some time. In 1847, Hugh moved the family to St. Louis, Missouri, where Elizabeth married John Keckley, a scoundrel and probable fugitive slave. Hugh wrote and had published a book about the life of John Randolph, which sold very well. But as the family was struggling to pay expenses, Elizabeth's income was a necessity. It seems that Elizabeth made many friends of both races, both free and enslaved, so she approached Hugh Garland with a request that she be allowed to purchase her freedom.

Garland was in the midst of preparing the appeal to the Missouri State Court of Appeals regarding the Dred Scott decision by an earlier court. But he set the price at $1,200. With the help of her friends and customers, she paid for the freedom of herself and her son George in November 1855. She promised to repay the loan from her friends, so she stayed in St. Louis. In early 1859, she moved to Baltimore, Maryland, began work as a seamstress and also began a school to teach her art of being a good seamstress, along with her special style of preparing and cutting.

In late summer 1860, she moved to Washington City, to find work but didn't have the money for a seamstress license. She finally acquired the license and began her seamstress business, and on March 4, 1861, she was introduced to Mary Todd Lincoln. She was invited to come to the White House for an interview for a position with the first lady on March 5, 1861. She was hired and worked as her personal dresser for the next six years.

Another Burwell daughter, Letitia Burwell (1850–1912), of the Berry Hill Plantation, south of Clarksville, visited New York as a child and was smitten. Following the war, she married and returned to New York sometime around 1880. There she became a successful writer. One of her novels, published in 1895, was *A Young Girl's Life in the South: Before the War.*

Right Reverend
John Stark Ravenscroft

Many books have been written about the "Old English Church" (the Episcopal Church) in the United States, Virginia and North Carolina, and most of these include chapters on Ravenscroft. But little has been written about his days in Christiansville. Ravenscroft was born in the spring of 1772 (research has three different dates) to John Ravenscroft and Lillias Miller of Petersburg. Completing his schooling in 1789 at age seventeen, he entered William and Mary College in the fall of that year. While living in Williamsburg, he met the Burwell family. He came to Christiansville to attend a christening of Lewis and Elizabeth Burwell's new daughter in 1791, and he received a conversion to the faith. Following this, he returned to William and Mary and excelled in his studies, graduating in 1793.

Ravenscroft and Ann Spotswood Burwell were married on August 13, 1792. Following his graduation, they moved to Christiansville to claim their dower: a three-hundred-acre parcel on Lunenburg Courthouse Road (today Highway 49), two miles north of the Meherrin River in Lunenburg County. That same year, their home, "Ravenscroft Manor," was built by master mason John Shelor and master carpenter John Inge. The home, sometimes referred to as "Magnolia Grove" and often, erroneously, as "Ravenswood," was two stories, with two rooms on each floor on either side of a large hallway. Several room additions were added, beginning in 1827, and the home is occupied today.

The only church in the county, the "Old Church of England" Episcopal, began in Christiansville in 1766 by purchasing the old Lunenburg

Ravenscroft Manor was occupied in the early 1950s by the Chance C. Price family. On the porch are Tex and Rex with Elizabeth on the stairs. *Courtesy Lucille Price McKinney Glassco.*

Courthouse as its meeting place. The courthouse was located about three hundred yards to the west of Little Bluestone Creek. With the Revolutionary War and the sentiment of the local citizens against England, the church was all but closed. When Ravenscroft became involved with the Christiansville Episcopal church, it was in a state of disrepair. In the late 1790s, he had as much of the timbers and foundation as possible salvaged and moved, and he rebuilt the church building three hundred yards east of Little Bluestone Creek. It was situated next to the future Abbeyville Road, high atop a hill (today the former Ben Roberts property) on West Sycamore Street. It was often referred to as the "Oak Grove Episcopal Church." Much larger and finer than the old courthouse building (with a gallery at one end), when the church reopened around 1795, it was well attended by the gentry planter families of the county. The congregation included nearly twenty-five members of the Burwell family, along with Colonel Samuel Goode and family, the Cunninghams, Puryears, Colemans, Baskervills, Bacons, Sturdivants, Olivers and others.

The church became very powerful very quickly and, by 1810, served as the Christiansville Community schoolhouse. But with the Civil War, members of the gentry lost their wealth. Many lost their families and homes, and many moved to other areas to begin anew. The church was nearly vacant again. The church had been referred to as the "Old Church" until 1857 when the name changed.

Ravenscroft had meetings with Presidents Thomas Jefferson and John Adams. Both wrote of him often in their communications and histories. In 1809, his wife, Ann, died suddenly, and Ravenscroft was silent, locked in his home, for nearly three years. Like a phoenix, in 1812, he emerged "on fire." He held a great revival at the Christiansville church, which got the attention of Mayor John Nelson (son of Secretary Thomas Nelson of New York) and several of his sons (who were moving to Mecklenburg County). So moved was the community and church governing body that in 1816 he was appointed in charge of the Episcopal churches in Mecklenburg and Lunenburg Counties. In 1817, he was made a deacon and became a minister for the churches. One of his first acts as deacon was the dedication of a new Episcopal church at Cabin Point (today Jeffreys Junction).

Ravenscroft was part of a group of county leaders who organized and had chartered the Boydton Academy in 1820 with Reverend Cowan, president (Episcopal), and Alexander Boyd Jr., treasurer. Board members were Dr. William Pattillo, Dr. Thomas Goode, Dr. Howell L. Jeffries, Captain Beverly Sydnor, John W. Lewis, Boydton Attorney, Dr. Tingnal Jones, Edward Tarry, Charles Baskervill, John W. Jones, John Nelson Jr., Samuel Lockett and Dr. Alexander S. Field. The church at Cabin Point was eventually disassembled and reassembled in Boydton in 1840 and is still there.

In 1821, Ravenscroft was in charge of the St. James Parish (most all of Southside) and, with the aid of John Nelson Jr., began a fundraising campaign for a theological seminary at the Diocese of William and Mary. At the Episcopal convention in 1822, he reported that funds of $10,268.33 (the largest subscription was from Mecklenburg County of $2,025, and next was Richmond with $1,920) had been raised. Prior to the convention on

April 25, 1822, Ravenscroft took time to perform the marriage ceremony at Prestwood Plantation for John Cole and Salina Skipwith.

At the close of the convention, Ravenscroft was nominated and selected to become the bishop of the Diocese of the North Carolina Episcopal Church. In 1823, Right Reverend Ravenscroft assumed his new position. Many of his sermons were copied, bound and published. He held the position of bishop until his death on January 14, 1830. There were no children that I could find from his marriage, but it appears that Ravenscroft Manor was still occupied after his departure, as a wing was built on either side of the manor in 1827.

Ravenscroft's will tells a great deal about the man who moved to North Carolina. He listed a number of conditions, to be met at his death. Some of the more remarkable were:

- His body was to be buried at Chancel of Christ Church, Raleigh, under the communion table, with a marble tablet to be mounted on the north wall, next to the pulpit, giving his name, age, office and time of death only.
- He was involved in a lawsuit in Richmond against Alexander Boyd, with respondents of John S. Hawkins and Blair Burwell. Confident of a victory, he wanted the sizable proceeds to go to the two children in Virginia "I have raised as my own": Alexander and Ebenezer McHarg Hepbourn. He also wanted his aged servant "Johnson" to have his horse "Pleasant."
- His homes in Fayetvil, Raleigh and Lunenburg County were to be sold and the monies given to the diocese.
- His personal belongings were sent to people in seven states, and he wanted his robes preserved for the new bishop. His extensive book collection was also to go to the diocese.
- Lastly, he stated that he had preserved his writings, letters and other correspondence, papers, manuscripts, journals, all transactions, sermons and public and private addresses. He wanted the church to publish all these into bound volumes.

His will was recorded on March 31, 1831.

A few years passed before the disposal of the estate at auction, and Ebenezer Hepbourn was able to purchase Ravenscroft Manor. In 1850, Hepbourn hired a farm overseer named Phillip Wallace, of Lunenburg County. Wallace (1826–1881), with his wife and five children, moved to the manor house, and on November 10, 1852, their son Lucious T. Wallace was born. Following his father's death in 1885, Lucious T. Wallace moved to the newly established Chase City in Mecklenburg County. There, he began working in the tobacco market. He became a tobacco broker and tobacconist with his partner, Robert M. Jeffreys. In 1901, Lucious married Jeffreys's only surviving child, Cora F. (1879–1936). Returning from their honeymoon, they moved into their new home, reported to be the first brick home in Chase City and was located on Boyd Street. They had four children.

After the war, a pillar of the Episcopal Church was S.N. Walker, father of Dr. C. Wesley Walker. He had purchased parcels and lots in Chase City from George Endly. In 1888, Walker gave a lot across the street from his home, at Marshall and Fourth Streets, to the church. The old church was dismantled, moved and rebuilt on its current location (though much smaller in size).

It was stated that in 1840, Burwells could be found in every state and territory in the United States. Also, in 1892, Dr. H.L. Burwell was in possession of Colonel Lewis Burwell's Revolutionary War sword.

Ravenscroft Manor is privately owned and still occupied today.

JOHN PURYEAR

CHRISTIANSVILLE AND PURYEAR'S STORE

In 1746, the newly formed county of Lunenburg needed a courthouse. William Puryear, a new settler to the local area, came to Lunenburg with a governor's land grant and settled on Little Bluestone Creek (at that time named Courthouse Branch). Next to his property, a courthouse was built. In 1765, when Mecklenburg County and Charlotte County were created from Lunenburg County, the courthouse building was no longer needed and the courthouse community was relocated. The newly formed counties quickly grew in population, as the area was vast, rich in several types of ore, had abundant wildlife and fertile soil and contained many rivers and streams. One of the first families to arrive in the newly formed Mecklenburg County was the nephew of William Puryear, John Puryear Sr. (1748–1785).

The Puryear family had come to the New World from the Alsace region of France (Huguenots). Both William and John originally settled in Warwick County, Virginia, but were offered the grants to aid in the westward expansion. In 1765, John received a grant for 1,575 acres of land, east and west of Butcher's Creek, east and west of Church Creek and adjoining the land of his uncle William. The original road in the area was a simple horse-and-wagon trail that began at the old Lunenburg courthouse and meandered north through the countryside to Petersburg. Along this road, referenced as Cooks Road in old court records, about a mile north of the courthouse, Puryear built a store on high ground next to Church Creek.

About 1766, the field next to this store became the Christiansville Quarter Horse Race Track. The racetrack was developed and owned by

Alexander Boyd, William Baskervill and David Craddock (and it was very likely that William J. Pattillo was also a partner). The Puryear home became an ordinary, but then the courthouse was closed and subsequently purchased for use as an Episcopal church. Pattillo and Craddock formed a partnership, purchased a plot containing seventeen acres and opened a store bordering the Christiansville Quarter Horse Race Track property. In 1786, when the new courthouse was completed for the newly formed (1765) Mecklenburg County, the road connected Mecklenburg Courthouse to Lunenburg Courthouse and then followed the National Indian Trading Trail (Highway U.S. 15 today) north through Keysville to Prince Edward County Courthouse and then to Petersburg. This trail has also been called the Syracuse to Savannah Trading Route.

John Puryear was an ambitious individual. Quickly, he built a home for his family atop a hill near the center of the northern boundary of his land. He built a gristmill and, on nearby Butcher's Creek, a tavern and store next to his home. In short order, he had acquired over twenty slaves, which had moved him up in the class structure to gentry planter. (The title "gentry" indicated one of substantial means and intelligence, so he made decisions and didn't do the physical labor. Basic requirements for that status were that the person must own over one thousand acres and more than twenty slaves. Owners of fewer than five hundred acres were classed as yeomen, and those owning somewhere between the two were referred to as planters.) He was classified as a Patriot during the Revolutionary War and was awarded a land warrant for one hundred acres in 1785. John fathered six sons and three daughters but died of an illness at the age of thirty-seven. Aware of his impending death, he made a will in 1785, three months before he died. He divided his estate equally among the nine children, with the exception of Samuel, who must have been the eldest, as he was the administrator.

John's widow inherited an equal share of the land and the store, home, mill and still, but Samuel was to be in charge of the operations and receive a share of the income. Samuel (b. circa 1765) married the elder daughter of Clausel Clausel (a titled Huguenot and gentry planter), Francis, on January 17, 1786, and she was given in marriage by her brother, Richard Clausel. The Clausel family was from the area of the new Mecklenburg Courthouse, the community that became known as Easter's Meeting House. Samuel built a home next door to his mother, acquired a stage mail stop and became the postmaster for Puryer's store area. It appears that in 1792, his mother died unexpectedly. Samuel converted the home to a tavern/ordinary, and in 1793, his brother William (b. 1760) took over the business and became the postmaster.

In about 1796, William left Mecklenburg County and took his family south to an area known today as Athens, Georgia. Shortly after their arrival and completion of their new home, William was killed in 1797. It was suspected that one or more of his slaves committed the murder. His widow remained there until her death. Some years later, the home was removed, and a new government building was erected: city hall of Athens, Georgia.

The tiny community of Old Courthouse (Puryear's Store) was beginning to grow and flourish. In 1796, the Honorable John Cunningham purchased William Puryear's estate of 1,201 acres and built a new home, Woodvale, for his new bride. Before 1800, it seems that Cunningham, Burwell and Samuel Puryear had become partners in the Christiansville Quarter Horse Race Track, which was only a short walk from Cunningham and Puryear's homes. But this was short-lived. In 1800, following Burwell's death, Samuel leased his ordinary to John Raines, who had been operating an ordinary for Burwell in Finneywood. Raines, in turn, hired Samuel Christian to operate the tavern, and it was registered with the United States Postmaster General as Christiansville. Then, in 1801, Samuel Christian purchased a parcel of land from the estate of William Finch, moved the tavern onto the property and continued to operate it for two years. In 1803, after settling the Burwell estate, John Raines came to Christiansville. He took over operation of the tavern and postal service. The tavern, newly remodeled by Raines, was referred to as Raines Tavern by those who came to the races, but it remained in the community of Christiansville.

Of the three men, Samuel Puryear was the only one that was not considered part of the gentry class, as he only owned six slaves. Samuel became very interested in horse racing and horse breeding. So much so that in 1803 (or 1809, depending on conflicting records), when Sir Patrick Edgar Nesbitt came to Christiansville to do research for his book on horse pedigree, Nesbitt stayed with Samuel for over a year and served as a tutor for the children of Samuel and Francis. Sir Edgar would leave for short periods of time to visit the local gentry planters and document their Thoroughbred and quarter horses, especially those belonging to the notable John Randolph of Roanoke Plantation in Charlotte County. If Sir Edgar came across a horse that he felt was being abused, he would simply take the horse and bring it home for Samuel to take care of.

In 1809, Puryear sold the store to William Birchette. The ordinary became known as Puryear's Gentleman's House (probably so dubbed by Sir Edgar) to distinguish it from Raines Tavern. The Gentleman's House was where all the gentry would meet to discuss business of the community. Samuel began to teach his sons, Richard Clausel and Alexander B., about horses, breeding and racing, as well as tavern, ordinary and mill operations so they could become skilled businessmen. His teachings seemed to be worthwhile. By 1811, Alexander Puryear and Company was a recognized successful business in Mecklenburg County and continued in operation for ten years.

During the War of 1812, Richard served as a private (as did his cousins John and Thomas Puryear) in 1814 under the command of Captain William Birchette. In 1815, Richard became the postmaster of the Christiansville post office and Alexander became postmaster of the new Greensborough post office. As part of the postal service of the day, they also operated a community store.

Both brothers married. In 1816, Richard (spring 1796–late fall 1863) married a woman apparently from the family of Bacon of Charlotte County, and on June 30, 1815, Alexander (circa 1780–1836) married Pollie (legally, Mary A.) Edwards (formerly of Granville County, North Carolina). Polly was living on the Greensborough plantation with her father, Peter Edwards, who had married Patsy R. Greenwood (and was now entitled to one-fifth of the family estate). By 1820, Samuel had joined the ranks of the gentry planters, with over one thousand acres of land, twenty horses and over twenty slaves. (As an aside, one of his slaves was a woman named Mariah. She was featured in 2010 on the television show *Who Do You Think You Are?* After Samuel's death, Mariah was deeded to his daughter, who subsequently took her to Alabama and gave her to Alexander, who had relocated there. Alexander was a slave trader at the time, but Mariah, who was allowed to marry, and her family became his personal servants. It is suspected by this writer that Alexander was her father. Mariah was the maternal great-great-great-grandmother for the famous NFL star Emmitt Smith of the Dallas Cowboys and winner of *Dancing with the Stars* in 2008.)

By 1818, Christiansville could boast that it had two gristmills; two stills; St. James Episcopal Church; two ordinaries; a tavern; a horse racetrack; Marshall & White, wagon makers and repairs; Hill & Wall, blacksmith shop; two attorneys; three retired colonels; a retired general; Hinton & Brame Co.; Deming & Co.; Craddock & Patillo, general store; Raines store; Brewer & Co.; Finch & Smith, tobacconist; a post office; and Captain Wm. Birchette & Co., real estate, among others. Becoming aware that he was going to die soon, in 1826, Samuel did something unusual: instead of leaving a will, he had a deed drawn to divide his properties among his children, with very calculated designations. Prior to his death, the Christiansville Quarter Horse Race Track was closed.

RICHARD CLAUSEL PURYEAR

"THE CITY"

R ichard left his position as postmaster in 1816 to live with his new bride, but he and Alexander returned to Christiansville in 1820. They resided at the tavern while they began a series of financial transactions. They formed a partnership to purchase the general store at the intersection of Boydton Courthouse Road and the newly created Abbeyville Road one mile south of the tavern. They also formed a partnership with Humberston Skipwith to purchase two Thoroughbred racehorses. Due to the ill health of his wife, probably due to the birth of their daughter Sara, Richard returned home in 1821 but then returned to Christiansville in 1822 and was reinstated as postmaster to serve a term of fifteen years (in 1836, that was extended for a period of thirty additional years). He held this position until his death in the fall of 1863. After his death, part of his personal inventory included the postal mailbox organizer, located in his home.

Richard married into a prosperous family because, when he returned to Christiansville, his children did not. (They must have remained with their grandparents.) He and his first wife, Elizabeth, who died sometime after 1825, had three children who survived: Richard R. (1818–June 1887), John Bacon (b. 1825) and Sara Francis Puryear, who later married Albert G. Jeffries of Charlotte County. In 1822, Richard Puryear & Co. was formed with business partners Achilles Jeffries, Richard Russell and Zachariah Bugg, but the business ceased operation in 1830. Richard quickly achieved gentry standing, with over twenty slaves and several thousand acres of land in Virginia and North Carolina in Granville, Warren and Randolph Counties.

Part of this included a 1,200-acre dower plantation from the Bacon family, in Finneywood, mostly located in Charlotte County.

When his father died in 1827 and the estate was settled, Richard took over as head of the planters' business meetings. He moved into the family home, the Puryear's Gentleman's House, with his mother, and took over operation of the ordinary and the store. Since the gentry planters controlled the finances of the Piedmont Region, they were opposed to a structured government locally. After all, Thomas Jefferson (who was opposed to big government, at any level) and family were in the neighborhood, and Monticello was only eighty miles north. It also appears that to distract from organizing Christiansville, the gentry began to purchase real estate and businesses in an effort to develop the chartered communities of Boydton and Clarksville.

In 1822, Captain William Birchette and his wife, Ann, sold Raines Tavern to John Raines, who had leased it in 1800 and then managed it for several years beginning in 1803 and was now living in Cumberland County, Virginia. Three months later, Raines, in turn, sold the tavern and land to Richard Puryear. By the close of 1822, Richard had acquired 1,356 acres of his grandfather's original tract. He also owned the 288-acre Christiansville tract with the tavern and the old quarter horse track. By 1830, along with his friends/business associates William Birchette and John (son of James) Cunningham, he was serving as assistant commissioner of revenue for the county. These three began a land acquisitions company and, by 1835, had purchased several parcels along the Boydton and Abbeyville Roads.

In 1834, with his gentry status and newly earned prosperity, Richard had Puryear's Gentleman's House moved to the intersection of the Boydton and Abbeyville Roads (which was developing and being referred to as "The City"), just across the Boydton Road from his (and Alexander's) store. He hired master carpenters to remodel the home into a more suitable accommodation for himself and his new bride, Mary A. Pettus, whom he married in 1834 and who was the daughter of Gentleman Justice Cephus Pettus.

Alexander, on the other hand, really liked the horse races. Friends with the Swepsons, Baskervills, Clausels and Goodes of Boydton, Alexander spent a lot of time at the Haymarket Thoroughbred Race Track in Boydton. He seemed to do very well at the track until 1820, and he made several land purchases in Virginia and North Carolina (or won the land in wagers) and built a tavern in Clarksville in 1820. Also in 1820, the Haymarket track was purchased by Colonel William Townes. In 1821, Alexander had accumulated a number of debts to friends and family. Many filed suit, and liens were

Shadow Lawn/Puryear's Gentleman's House following remodeling by Jacob Holt in 1870. *Courtesy Glen and Lisa Gillispie.*

placed on his holdings. By 1824, he had lost the tavern, had several notes due and had bet Polly's inheritance in the Greensborough Plantation.

Alexander had also lost the store and his position as postmaster. He and Polly relocated to her family's plantation in Granville County, but soon his creditors from Mecklenburg County were filing suit there also. In December 1831, Alex returned to Mecklenburg County, and several of his lawsuits were dismissed. Then, with the help of Richard Puryear and Humberston Skipwith, Alex gathered a group of slaves and moved to Madison County, Alabama. There he became a slave trader throughout Alabama and Louisiana.

While construction was underway on Puryear's Gentleman's House, it appears Richard and his new wife honeymooned by traveling extensively through North Carolina (probably inspecting their properties) and visiting Alexander in Burnt Corn, Alabama. Before their return, Richard acquired lands in Mississippi, Louisiana and Texas. When they returned, Puryear's Gentleman's House was opened for business in "The City." A large spring well was dug in the front yard for the family and guests.

An orchard was planted across the road, to the left of the front door and behind the store. Also across the road was a pasture so Richard could admire his thoroughbred and quarter horses. Household servants and slave quarters were to the north and west of the home, but some household servants lived in a room under the staircase.

In 1836, Richard's brother, Alexander, died, leaving his estate to Richard with provisions for his wife, Polly, with Richard as her administrator. Alexander and Polly had no children. Richard returned to Alabama for a few months to settle the estate. In 1838, Richard and Mary Puryear had their first child, Elizabeth. As a child, Elizabeth was enamored of the wealth and style of the citizens of Christiansville, spurred in part, I'm sure, by the fact that her father was a school commissioner for the district for a time and was in charge of the state literary fund for the county. She seemed to love learning and wrote about her time in Christiansville later in life. She remarked about the stories told by General Keen and Colonel Levi (their neighbors), the fine carriages of the Cunninghams and Burwells, the Centenary School and the orchards and gardens, which all spurred her quest to learn. Interestingly, she never wrote about the horses or tobacco and only admiringly mentioned the household slaves, who were regarded as family members.

Around 1841, Richard C.'s son, Dr. Richard R. Puryear, came to Christiansville and moved into Puryear's Gentleman's House. He, with his partner, Dr. William F. Dodson, took over the practices of Drs. Bigger and Thomas Carden. Now not only did Elizabeth have a new half brother, but in 1841, the house was a bustling residence, hosting Richard C.; his wife, Mary; daughter Elizabeth, age three; as well as a one-year-old and a newborn. In addition, there was Dr. Richard R., age twenty-three, with his medical office in the home, which was still an ordinary and an office for Richard C. to conduct his businesses, and it was still serving as a mail stagecoach stop and meeting place for the gentry. Interesting, in January 1846, the youngest of the three children by Richard's first marriage, John Bacon Puryear, appeared in circuit court in Mecklenburg County and requested that Albert Jeffries be appointed his guardian (although he was age twenty and Albert was his brother-in-law).

Puryear was a gifted businessman, investing in the first bateaux shipping company on the Roanoke River. The company had to dig canals and build dams starting in Weldon, North Carolina, and it was owned, in part, by Richard and several family members. In the latter 1840s, his real estate company continued to acquire properties, including the Boydton Hotel/Tavern in 1849, and in 1850, he was a principal in building the Boydton Savings Bank. On the 1850 census record, his son John Bacon Puryear is listed as residing in the Boydton Hotel with a stated occupation of merchant at age twenty-five. In April 1853, John B. was sworn in as a deputy sheriff, serving with High Sheriff Reuben A. Puryear Sr., his cousin.

Richard C. Puryear was one of the most respected men in the county. The Mecklenburg County Circuit Court record, dated July 19, 1858, states that "R.C. Puryear, one of the firm of Cogbill, Johnson & Co., has appeared in court and took the oath prescribed by law in relation to his dealing with slaves and free negroes in selling wine and ardent spirits in the county." Shortly after this, Sir Patrick Nesbitt returned to Christiansville to compile more data on a second volume for his pedigree horse registry. He stayed at the Gentleman's House and again served as a tutor for the children.

Under Puryear's leadership, "The City" continued to grow and prosper. In 1850, Colonel John F. Finch and his brother Edward Jr. built a tobacco factory at the southeast corner of the junction. Next door, Colonel Finch built a fine home that still stands today.

The Finch brothers then went to Clarksville and built a second factory. With the great fire of 1858 in Clarksville, there was damage to the factory and the Finch bothers leased it in 1860. With the beginning of the Civil War, both factories were closed. In 1868, when George Endly came to town and purchased 1,350 acres of Puryear's Plantation (including "The City"), the old Finch tobacco factory served as the Presbyterian church until a new sanctuary could be built.

Just before the war, around 1860, Dr. James Walker and his partner, Dr. W.G. Oliver, arrived in "The City." Dr. Walker purchased a fifty-acre parcel encompassing the southwest quadrant at the intersection of Abbeyville and Boydton Roads, where he built a home and established a medical practice. He and Dr. Oliver took over the practices of Drs. Puryear and Cunningham.

The last documented trip Richard C. made to Alabama was in 1857, when he was sixty-four. It appears that he went to divest his holdings in Alabama and North Carolina. Despite the uprisings over slavery and states' rights in the south, he went but with fear in his heart. Before leaving home, he had written a will with his last wishes, and he wrote as if he would not return. He also wrote and filed a power of attorney, naming his son John Bacon as his representative. He returned to "The City" in 1858. He was just in time for his daughter Elizabeth's wedding to her cousin Thomas T. Pettus, of the Corn Hill Plantation. In April 1863, the court had put him in charge of the elections to be held at Christiansville Tavern, and at some point after April, John Bacon Puryear left the county. It appears that he traveled to Alabama, most likely to take care of Aunt Polly, who soon died. He was unable to return to Christiansville for his father's funeral or to administer the estate in the fall of 1863. Following the war, he returned to Charlotte County, where he worked as a teacher until his death on July 18, 1878.

When the Commonwealth of Virginia voted to secede, Richard C. was there, representing the Southside District. Upon his return to "The City," he immediately helped organize a recruitment center at the Christiansville Academy and Raines Tavern. He was also active in the Senior Home Guard Unit in Christianville. At the age of sixty-eight, he was still first in line to defend his beloved Christiansville community. During the war, Elizabeth returned home while her husband went off to fight. She had three children when she returned home to assist her father. Richard's will does not list his real estate holdings through the land company or in other states, but his personal holdings in the Christiansville community alone during the depression of 1864 and in war-torn Virginia would still be valued today at several million dollars, making him the second-wealthiest gentry planter in the county at that time. The will also did not list his slaves, horses, cash or personal property, but his son Dr. Richard and son-in-law Albert had to post a $250,000 bond each to administer the estate.

I'M SEEING DOUBLE

RICHARD CLAUSEL PURYEAR (SON OF JOHN)

I would be remiss if I didn't mention the difficulty in doing historical research. Over a period of several years, I had compiled a lot of information on Richard Clausel Puryear, but much of the information didn't match. One person by this name appeared to live in North Carolina but owned property in Southside Virginia, and the other seemed to live in Southside Virginia but owned property in North Carolina. Then I discovered there were two. Samuel Puryear had a brother, John (1772–1809). John married the younger daughter of Clausel Clausel, Sarah (Sally) Shepherd Clausel, on October 24, 1799. She was given in marriage by her older brother, Hezekiah Clausel. From this marriage, there was only one child born, Richard Clausel Puryear (February 9, 1801–July 30, 1867). John received a large dower for the marriage, consisting primarily of lands in North Carolina.

After the marriage, the couple resided in Mecklenburg County for over six years in order to take care of the ailing Clausel Clausel. But they, too, seemed to be in poor health. When they moved to North Carolina, they left Richard Clausel Puryear with John's younger sister, Elizabeth. At the time, she was living and working as a teacher in Huntsville, North Carolina. John and Sarah had a home built in Brookstown, North Carolina, in 1806, on the east bank of the Yadkin River. They owned over one thousand acres of land along the river and Little Yadkin Creek in Stokes County, North Carolina. They also inherited five slaves with the property.

Before they moved from Mecklenburg County, tragedy struck the home of Clausel Clausel. His wife died in 1804, and she had inherited the property of her mother, who had just died a short time before that. Then Clausel Clausel died on March 13, 1806. His will assigned all his holdings, his wife's holdings, the holdings of his wife's parents and the dower holdings of Lucinda (widow of his oldest son) to John Puryear. In 1809, at the age of thirty-seven, John died in Stokes County. He left the entire fortune to his only son, Richard Clausel Puryear. Sally went on to marry Frances Rose of the Piedmont area of Virginia (most likely Brunswick County). He was the son of Captain Howell Rose, who had land holdings in Mecklenburg County and Granville County.

Richard was educated in a classical fashion by Aunt Elizabeth, and he pursued further classical studies with teachers at private schools in North Carolina. He married Elizabeth Ann Clingman (b. circa 1825), who was the daughter of Peter and Jane Poindexter Clingman of Virginia. From this marriage, they had three children. The firstborn was a son named (you'd never guess) Richard Clausel Puryear II, while the second son was named Thomas Puryear and the third child was a daughter, Bettie Pattillo Puryear. Betty (b. circa 1842) went on to marry William Gibson, and they lived until 1927.

Richard served as an elected magistrate for Surry County, North Carolina, and was later elected a colonel in the regional North Carolina militia. He went on to serve three terms in the North Carolina House of Commons and one term in the North Carolina Senate. He was later elected to and served two terms in the United States Congress. With the talks of secession and its eventual occurrence, Richard was elected to serve the Piedmont Region of North Carolina as a congressman to the first provisional Congress of the Confederate States, originally slated to be held in Raleigh, North Carolina, but changed to Richmond, Virginia. While there, Richard Clausel Puryear of Piedmont North Carolina sat next to the Sixth District congressman from Piedmont Virginia—Richard Clausel Puryear.

In 1865, Richard Clausel Puryear of North Carolina was elected to attend the Peace Accord in Philadelphia, and in 1867, he died. Both men were equally wealthy, and they were both gentry planters with extensive holdings. They both were instrumental in establishing schools, both were in the militia and both were devoutly loyal to the South. One slight distinction: Richard Clausel Puryear of Christiansville named his firstborn son Richard R.

SIR PATRICK EDGAR NESBITT

THE FAMOUS THOROUGHBREDS AND QUARTER HORSES

A man of many names, Sir Patrick Edgar Nesbitt (Nesbett/Nisbitt)—or Patrick Edgar, Eddie Ochiltree or Patrick Edgar-Nesbitt—was born in 1770 in Dublin, Ireland, the son of Patrick and Margaret Edgar. His father was a prosperous merchant and provided for his education at the University of Dublin. Reportedly, Edgar was an eccentric and had a fiery temper. He was accused of killing the family gardener. After his father died in 1794, he escaped from Ireland (apparently he was wanted for the murder) and came to the United States around 1800, arriving first in North Carolina and then going to Virginia. He taught children in exchange for room and board, a stipend and access to plantation owners with Thoroughbred racehorses. Nesbitt, also a writer about the sporting horses, had published several articles for magazines of the day.

The first record of him being in Southside Virginia is in 1803. He left his position in North Carolina and came to the home of Colonel William Townes, where he taught the children for about a year. The next record is that he taught the children of Samuel Puryear, who owned an ordinary next to the Christiansville Quarter Horse Race Track, in 1809 for over a year. (In some records these two are switched, indicating that he worked for Townes in 1809 and Puryear in 1803.) While there, if Nesbitt went to a horse breeder he didn't like and thought the breeder didn't understand horses, he would take the horse in question. He would then bring it to Christiansville and give it to Samuel. While in Christiansville, he visited the stables of John Randolph, Burwell and others.

The first data he collected and recorded was from Allen Young Sr., circa 1803, of Cox and Allen's Creek, in Mecklenburg County, Virginia. The Piedmont region on both sides of the Roanoke River was referred to in the early nineteenth century as the "Old Race Horse Region." In 1811, Nesbitt was teaching and living in Greenville County, Virginia. Around 1820, he did own one blooded horse: Rossetta, formerly owned by William Byrd III of Westover. Next, in 1822, he went to Captain James Junkin Harrison (1780–1851), of "Diamond Grove" on the Meherrin River in Brunswick County, Virginia. While there, he was selected by Harrison to prepare a book on the Thoroughbred bloodlines. Nesbitt began gathering data under Harrison's supervision for publication in a book. Nesbitt stayed in the Piedmont region for the remainder of his life because, at some point, most of the great horses of Thoroughbred bloodlines were at stud here and these records with the names of their fold were readily available to him. He also recorded some of the quarter horse ancestry from such great Thoroughbred names of the eighteenth century as Janus, Polly Williams and One Eye.

Other horses of note included Babram, Monkey, Silver Eye, Jolly Roger and Mark Anthony. The primary breeders of the Piedmont were Thomas Field, John Goode, William Davis, Henry Delony and Peyton Skipwith of Mecklenburg County, Virginia; John Alston and Willie Jones of Halifax County, North Carolina; Charles Eaton and Wm. Mills of Granville County, North Carolina; Colonel Thomas Eaton and Marmaduke Johnson of Warren County, North Carolina; and Colonel Lewis Burwell, Colonel William Townes and William Baskervill of Mecklenburg County, with additional holdings in Warren and Granville Counties, North Carolina. The names of John Randolph and the Carrington family of Charlotte County, along with the Bruces of Halifax County, have to be included in this list.

In 1820, Colonel William Townes became the owner of Haymarket Race Track and the Boyd Tavern, in Boydton, both of which he operated until 1828, when he closed the racetrack. A lover of the sporting horse, he began the Roanoke Basin Colt Association. Partnering with Townes was Delegate George R. Rogers, and they hosted many public events and celebratory dinners at the tavern (which Townes had remodeled into a hotel). Probably the most significant was the Roanoke Colt Show on June 20, 1839, with participants coming from as far away as New York. This was the first notable Thoroughbred colt auction in Southside since closing the Newmarket Race Track in 1828. It is reported to have continued as an annual event for several years.

Following the closing of the Newmarket Race Track in 1828, Nesbitt relocated to Williamsboro, Granville County, North Carolina. Having published articles in the *Sportsman Herald* and other sporting horse magazines during the 1820s and early 1830s, finally in 1833 he had his book published. Nesbitt was regarded by the publisher, Henry Mason of New York, as the "father of the American Turf." Mason published *The American Turf Register* for Patrick Nisbett Edgar & Co. from Vance County, North Carolina. Nesbitt was said to have completed a second volume before his death, but it was never located and considered to have been either lost or destroyed during one of Nesbitt's tantrums. Racetracks were found throughout Southside, with multiple quarter-mile tracks in most communities and at least two Thoroughbred tracks, one each in Mecklenburg and Halifax Counties, Virginia. All were closed by 1830 except the one in Halifax County, which operated the longest (until sometime after 1875).

In 1839 and 1840, Nesbitt was teaching at a home in the Tar River District of Granville County, North Carolina. Then he returned to Christiansville and taught Richard Clausel Puryear's children around 1845. It is almost certain, based on a letter from Richard's daughter in 1888, that Nesbitt provided lectures at the Christiansville Academy during his stay.

The 1850 census listed Nesbitt's age as eighty and recorded him as living in Granville County, North Carolina, in the home of James Currin, age twenty-five, with his wife and children. The Currin home was located in the Abraham's Planes District. The local history is that Nesbitt, at the age of eighty-seven, was out for a horseback ride through the countryside and got caught in a snowstorm. He died of exposure on October 27, 1857, on or near Dr. David Jiggetts's plantation near St. Tammany on the Roanoke River. (There is a notation that he is buried in the Jiggetts family cemetery.) He was considered the foremost authority on Thoroughbred horses of the time but with some omissions (if he didn't like the horse owner, he didn't list him).

The inventory of his estate in North Carolina is also listed in Will Book 20, pages 501–3, Granville County, North Carolina. A. Sandis was appointed executor of the estate in Granville County. On the inventory, a number of books, toilet items, clothing and horse gear were listed. These sold at auction for a total of $169.49.

On December 21, 1857, his estate in Mecklenburg County was turned over to William Baskervill Jr. as administrator. It was then turned over to the sheriff for probate. Because Nesbitt was found and treated in Mecklenburg County, and was thus a resident when he died, his case was turned over to the commonwealth's attorney, Thomas F. Goode. An inventory was conducted and filed with the court. It was also posted in the county will books, like Granville County had done.

Cash	$28.75
Saddle and horse	69.00
5 shares of bank bonds @ $104	$520
Acct. of R.V. Gaired	$2,500
" " "	783.63 accrual interest
" " "	360.87 interest accrued from Jan 1, 1859 to pres. (Jul., 1860)
Total	$4,262.25

EXPENSES:

General	$125.85
Coffin	20
Thos. F. Goode	5
Charlotte & c	21.37
Tickets & c	2.50
S.P. Thrower	39.32
Publication	1.75
Tax on a/c	21.91
Co. tax on a/c	14.00
BALANCE OF ESTATE	$4,136.40

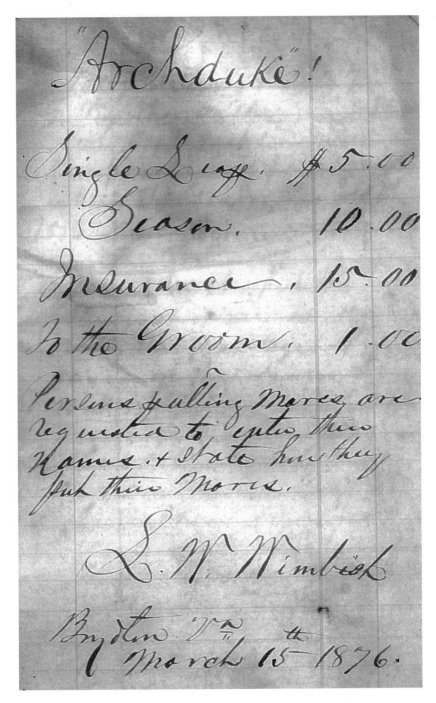

The 1876 studbook for Archduke during his stand at the Lewis Wimbish plantation in Boydton. *Courtesy William C. Gregory.*

An affidavit was received in the circuit court of Mecklenburg County for Maria Edgar, sister, for the estate of Patrick Edgar. The affidavit was filed with the court by her attorney, Elijah Satterwhite, on March 8, 1860 (she was in Ireland), along with a power of attorney authorizing Satterwhite to represent her. Sheriff William A. Blanch was placed in charge of disposing of the estate. On August 20, 1860, Edgar's estate was returned to Commissioner Walker, and on September 17, 1860, the court ruled that it was settled.

Following the war, with literally hundreds of thousands of horses having been killed, Thoroughbred horses became almost extinct in the Piedmont. Thoroughbred jockeys and trainers left their families in the Piedmont and migrated to Kentucky and Tennessee. Most local breeders turned their attention to a working stock of horses. However, there were two notable exceptions: Colonel John T. Goode and Dr. Robert D. Baskervill. In 1875, Baskervill put out his Thoroughbred stallion, Archduke, to stud, at the plantation of Lewis Wimbish.

FERRY HILL PLANTATION AND THE FIRST COMMISSIONED TOBACCO INSPECTOR FOR SOUTHSIDE

CAPTAIN WILLIAM BIRCHETTE (BURCHETT)

C lark Royster is the namesake for and credited with the patenting, platting and developing of the community of Clarks Town, which became Clarksville. He inherited a 376-acre parcel of land from his father, from which he platted twenty-five lots and twenty-five parcels to be sold and a 50-acre plot for his personal use. He began to speculate by purchasing property surrounding the area, and then he applied to the Virginia General Assembly for a charter for his town, which was granted in 1818. New development for the community was very slow, and Royster found himself in serious financial difficulty, with some of his properties in foreclosure. At this juncture, the businessmen from Christiansville began to purchase lots and parcels. The Land Company of Puryear and Birchette purchased a number of lots and several parcels in the platted town of Clarksville to assist Royster with achieving solvency. Much of the support Royster had counted on chose to move with Colonel William Townes to Boydton. There, they purchased the Boydton Hotel and built and developed the Newmarket Thoroughbred Horse Race Track. Even John Speed sold Buffalo Springs Resort and relocated to Boydton.

Adjoining the lands of Royster was the plantation and vast land holdings of Sir Peyton Skipwith, Prestwood Plantation, which encompassed about four thousand acres that he had purchased. It was a parcel of the Colonel William Byrd patent, including the Bluestone Castle, which had been built for Byrd by his overseer. Skipwith had the castle removed and built Prestwood around 1795 using the same carpenters and masons who built Ravenscroft. In 1806,

The Boyd Tavern, circa 1790, in Boydton, Virginia. Site of filming of NBC's *Who Do You Think You Are?* in 2008. The author and Emmitt Smith are pictured with film crews in front. *Courtesy Boyd Family Foundation, Jack Hite, president.*

Skipwith died, and the court appointed John Cunningham of Christiansville as the administrator of the estate and trustee of Lady Jane Skipwith. Lady Jane entrusted him not only with the management of the estate but also with the management of the store (the first recorded millinery in the county) and the horses. Since Cunningham was from Christiansville, much of the sales of goods and land holdings and racing of Skipwith's Thoroughbred horses took place there. The horses of Skipwith's estate would have raced against the great Thoroughbreds of the estate of Colonel Lewis Burwell, Samuel Puryear and other gentry planters, including Senator John Goode, George Baskerville and Colonel William Towns.

From these races and meetings, Clarksville began to flourish, with a navigation company on the Roanoke River to Townsville and Weldon, North Carolina, and new roads to Buffalo Springs Resort and on to Danville, Virginia, as well as new roads to Oxford and Roxboro, North Carolina. Developers such as the Vowels, Woods, Venables and Geoghegans began to arrive in the community, all purchasing lands in Mecklenburg County, Virginia, and in Granville and Person Counties, North Carolina. Soon, there was a prosperous tobacco market, probably the second-largest in the

Moss Tobacco Warehouse, Clarksville, circa 1848. This was the largest warehouse, with over forty resident employees, primarily free blacks from North Carolina. *Courtesy Bob Howerton.*

commonwealth (next to Petersburg). The first tobacco inspector, appointed by the governor of the state, was William Birchette in 1830 (though earlier appointments had been attempted).

A Huguenot by birth, William Birchette (1778–circa 1846) arrived in Christiansville, Virginia, around 1795. He, with his brothers, James and Richard, formed a partnership and began administering estates and purchasing land. They were also serving as independent bankers and making loans throughout the county. Within five years, they had purchased several large farms, followed in 1809 by the purchase of Raines Tavern. By 1812, William Birchette had become one of the largest tobacco farmers in northwest Mecklenburg County and was a member of the gentry planter class. As a member of the Christiansville Twenty-second Regiment Militia, Captain Birchette was called to duty during the War of 1812, primarily in the local area and Boydton. But in August 1814, he was activated into the army and ordered to report, with his company of men, to Yorktown and await further orders. He and his company (which included Private Richard C. Puryear) served for sixteen days in the army at Yorktown during the months of August and September. (With an Act of the U.S. Congress in July 1832, he and his men received land warrants in gratitude for their service. The acreage of the warrant was determined by the rank and length of service of each man.)

Upon his return to Christiansville, he was one of the organizing investors in the Roanoke Navigation Company of Clarksville and the Oxford to Clarksville Plank Road in 1818. That year, he purchased two tobacco farms in Boydton and another farm in Christiansville. With Royster in foreclosure in 1819, Birchette purchased the 1,201-acre tract from Colonel William Townes (who held the mortgage) referred to as "the ferry hill tract." The ferry hill tract joined Townes's property to the east and Skipwith's property to the west.

There, he built a new home for himself; his wife, Ann; and their children, and he petitioned the postmaster general and was granted approval for a post office in 1819. He licensed his home as an ordinary and tavern, which he operated for many years. The name Ferry Hill is somewhat misleading, as it was not on the Roanoke or the Dan Rivers. In fact, it was on a tributary stream, Sandy Creek, which fed into the Roanoke River. Often the low grounds of the rivers were flooded, so a ferry was established for the wide portion of the creek channel. Later, in the 1830s, a bridge was built across the creek on Colonel Townes plantation—Occoneechee—about five hundred yards east of the ferry landing.

The new bridge over the Dan River was completed in 1921 from First Street in Clarksville to Occoneechee Island. All this area is now under lake waters. *Courtesy Bob Howerton.*

In 1820, Birchette purchased ten lots in Clarksville and fifteen of the parcels from Clark Royster under the name of his new land company: Birchette and Company. On Virginia Avenue in Clarksville, Birchette and Company built a tavern and ordinary. The company also owned and operated a dry goods store next door. Then, the company purchased Raines Tavern in Christiansville (which Birchette had sold to Raines in 1814) but, three months later, sold it as a personal investment to Richard C. Puryear for a $100 profit. Within two years, Birchette and Company had built a stemming and prizery operation for the packaging and shipping of tobacco in Boydton. In 1822, when the Clarksville post office was opened for business, the postal service retained the name Ferry Hill for the community north of the rivers. In 1826, William Birchette's oldest brother, Richard, died.

Elected justice of the peace and presiding on the circuit court bench in Boydton, William Birchette served as the presiding justice for the Court of Oyer and Terminers in 1831 and 1832. In 1830, Birchette, along with James Cunningham (son of John) and Richard C. Puryear (son of Samuel), was appointed assistant county commissioner of revenue by the presiding justices of the circuit court. Also in 1830, Birchette received a gubernatorial appointment from Governor William Giles as the first tobacco inspector (later called auctioneer) of the Southside area. He chose to build a warehouse in Clarksville. (Today, Clarksville continues to boast that it is the oldest continuous tobacco market in the world, though more likely this should be the United States). Birchette and Company also built a new stemming factory and prizery in Clarksville.

For a man of many talents, appointments, acquired wealth and community standing, Birchette's name is rarely mentioned in history books or historical writings. When he died circa 1846, he had spent two years settling his holdings of interest bearing notes and much of his land with his sons, James and William, and a son-in-law, Joseph G. Snead. There was no recorded will. By 1848, most all of Birchette's children had married and moved to Granville and Warren Counties in North Carolina. There is some family lore from the Bullock family, in Granville County, North Carolina, that when the Roanoke Navigation Company was completed circa 1822 to Clarksville, Birchette's daughter Elizabeth Ann was one of the first passengers to leave Clarksville. She had married a William Bullock, whose lands were east of Townsville, Granville County, North Carolina. After all, Birchette was president of the company with David Shelton as treasurer.

Later, following the new federal government highway system in 1922, the Ferry Hill property was platted and became a part of a proposed community

The bridge over Grassy Creek, leading from Mecklenburg County to Granville County, during the flood of 1941. *Courtesy the late John Goode Taylor.*

Construction in progress on the powerhouse at the John H. Kerr Dam on the Roanoke River. *Courtesy U.S. Army Corps of Engineers, Wilmington District.*

of North Clarksville. Following the Depression in the early 1930s and the great flood of the Piedmont region in 1941, North Clarksville was abandoned as a project. The great flood of 1941 was the largest recorded in the history of the states of Virginia and North Carolina. Over sixty-five thousand acres were under water. Flood damage was found from Danville, Virginia, to Rocky Mount, North Carolina. The primary area of destruction was centered in the Southside area of Virginia, starting around South Boston, Halifax County, spreading throughout Mecklenburg County, parts of Brunswick County and moving across the border to northern Granville, Vance and Warren Counties on to Roanoke Rapids, North Carolina. It resulted in a devastating loss of property, infrastructure and livestock, as well as businesses and history. As a result of the flood, in 1944, the U.S. Army Corps of Engineers began the initial steps toward building the John H. Kerr Dam (named for a congressman from North Carolina) and Buggs Island Reservoir (Lake), named for Samuel Bugg III, one of the original seventeenth-century landowners of the Virginia area.

Aerial view of Clarksville with the twin bridges over Buggs Island Lake. Hot air balloons are common during town festivities. *Courtesy Lakeside Flight Service, Joel Noah.*

In recent years, Ferry Hill has been purchased by a development company and platted and parceled as a lakefront community. Between the lake and the subdivision, most all the history is gone.

SAMUEL TAYLOR TARRY (BIG SAM)

S amuel Tarry (1716–1765) came to Virginia from Middlesex, England, around 1739 and settled in Amelia County. He married Mary Booker (1711–1756). Following her death, and with five small children, he soon married Mary Crawley (d. 1764), and they had four children before she died. In 1760 and 1764, he purchased one thousand acres of land in the "new Virginia Lunenburg County," south of the Roanoke River. His two elder sons, George and Edward, purchased more land for the plantation from John Taylor, and it was named Ivy Hill.

George (1748–1816) was appointed and served as a colonel in the Twenty-second Regiment, Mecklenburg County militia. He married Sarah Taylor, the daughter of William Taylor. Their home, built next door to Ivy Hill, was named Long Grass and completed in 1782. They had four sons, and the third was named Samuel Taylor Tarry (1795–1849). Samuel T. became known as "Big Sam." At the death of his father, George, the plantation and fifty-six slaves were willed to the eldest son, Edwin C. Tarry.

George left Samuel T. a parcel of land and slaves, so he built a home called Wildwood. In his will, George left his wife, Sarah T., an equal share of the estate, property and slaves, and in addition, she was to share the title of the portion of the estate left to Samuel T. and would receive full ownership at his death. This might suggest that Samuel T. was not in the best of health.

According to the deed books, in the 1840s, Samuel T. was selling off future ownership of his home, furnishings and slaves. In 1846, a deed was recorded whereby he was attempting to settle nine debts that totaled about $755 in

The Ivy Hill Plantation manor house of Samuel Tarry, circa 1784, as seen in the 1933 photo collection of the late Herbert Hutcheson. *Courtesy of Richard Bland.*

exchange for future ownership of two horses, three wagons, two cows and calves, a crop of tobacco with the planting tools, household and kitchen furnishings and a crop of wheat that was growing. Also, a second deed was recorded in which he and his wife, Sarah C. (the only reference I found of a wife), were selling off the fifth of her dower in slaves, which was witnessed and certified by John Clardy and William Taylor. Samuel was also involved in business transactions in 1848

This view of the Long Grass Plantation manor house of George Tarry, circa 1790, is found in the 1933 photo collection of the late Herbert Hutcheson. *Courtesy of Richard Bland.*

with his cousin William W. Tarry, of the state of Alabama, county of Perry, and son of Edwin C. Tarry.

Apparently, due to his size, Samuel was exempt from militia service. There is no record that I found of his involvement in any activities of the county or community. After his home was built, he contracted with the local legend of chair making, Thomas Johnson (father of Warner Keeton Johnson), to have a special set of chairs made for his home (and probably other furniture). He also had special dishes and pottery, and his clothing was all custom made. Although ready-made clothes were not abundant in those days, what was available would not have been suitable. It was stated in family records that he was over seven feet tall and weighed over five hundred pounds.

Samuel T.'s brother George (1801–1884) married Mary Euphemia Hamilton, of Burnside, Granville County, North Carolina. Together, George and Mary

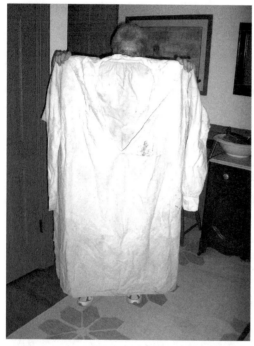

built their home near Ivy Hill, and it was named Long Grass Plantation. Their firstborn son at Long Grass was Samuel A. Tarry. On October 17, 1831, Samuel A. Tarry qualified as an ensign in the militia and was so certified by the court. He had married Mary A. Brame (b. March 14, 1808) on December 12, 1827, in Mecklenburg County, Virginia. He served as a justice of the county with his uncle George in the 1830s. The son, Samuel Tarry (b. circa 1834), of Samuel A. & Mary, attended the University of Virginia and finished his first year in 1857, having completed components of math, natural philosophy and chemistry.

Top: Samuel T. Tarry's shirt is being displayed by the owner, Mrs. Peyton Tarry, who is slightly taller than five feet. *Courtesy of Mark Anthony Pace.*

Left: Samuel T. Tarry's dress slacks are in possession of and being displayed by his great-great-great-great-niece, Mrs. Peyton Tarry, of Oxford, North Carolina. *Courtesy of Mark Anthony Pace.*

THE CHRISTIANSVILLE ACADEMY

A petition to the commonwealth of Virginia resulted in Christiansville Academy being chartered in Mecklenburg County, and it began operation in the fall of 1829. The original board of trustees included Peyton R. Burwell, Daniel Smith, Richard Russell, Richard Clausel Puryear (son of Samuel), William W. Smith, John Pettus, James May, Edward Dodson, Dabney Collier and John F. Finch, all of Mecklenburg County. The land for the school was a two-acre parcel next to the Episcopal Church on Abbeyville Road. It was purchased from Bartholomew and Ann Egan for ten dollars. There was a notation that the land was the former home of Bartholomew Egan (who must have been the previous minister to the church), which was being used as a schoolhouse before 1829. The stipulation was that the land could only be used for a school (as the building had already been built and had been in operation for at least three years), and in the future, if the school closed, the land would revert back to the Egans' heirs.

The first instructor and principal was Captain David Bigger of the Black Branch community. The academy opened as an all-male academy (as most all academies were segregated by the sexes in those days), and Bigger operated a traditional "classical studies" program of Latin, Greek, math, natural philosophy and moral philosophy. There were a number of individuals who assisted on a regular basis, and the local ministers were expected to take part in teaching, along with their music directors.

For culture and refinement, many of the gentry planters must have participated with lectures on planting, slave management, financial

SOUTHSIDE VIRGINIA CHRONICLES

administration and contemporary topics of interest. The planters were well read, with vast libraries, and many of their children and relatives' children were in attendance at the school. The planters were familiar with geography, as most owned property in multiple states and traveled frequently. A wide variety of politicians would deliver speeches when visiting relatives nearby, and entertainers would perform, including Joe Sweeney (known as "Mr. Banjo Man"). It was written that a number of artists from Richmond, Baltimore and Philadelphia were frequent lecturers and provided instruction.

From 1833 through 1835, a regular lecturer at the school was Dr. John William Draper, who had been educated at Wesleyan Academy and London University. He was a noted scholar and researcher. Draper could have lectured on natural science and geology, social science and world history. While living with his sister near Christiansville, he conducted laboratory experiments in the basement of their home. It is written that in that basement lab, he built the prototype for and thus invented the first camera. His legacy has filled many volumes of history. His sister Dorothy Catherine Draper also taught Anglo-Saxon and English literature and poetry. She, her sister and John began Drapers School for Girls in their home. They are also credited with establishing the Concord Meetinghouse for the Quaker community before 1830.

A fellow Englishman on the board of directors for the school was John May (b. 1812), who had been educated at Oxford in England. He was a regular lecturer on the classics and geography, as he had traveled extensively in other countries. With Randolph Macon College located nine miles south in Boydton, I would have to believe that some of the students (either those from Christiansville, those working for an *Artium Magister* degree and others) visited and lectured at the school.

By 1833, the very popular academy had grown to an extent that Captain Bigger felt he could no longer manage it, and he resigned. It appears his wife may also have been in poor health because in the circuit court records for January 17, 1859, Captain David J. Bigger was appointed executor of the estate of his wife, Sarah M. Bigger. He was replaced as principal of the academy by Methodist reverend Adam Finch (1804–1872), brother of the board member John F. Finch.

Adam Finch Sr. was born in Charlotte County, Virginia, on June 23, 1800. He married Mary A. Bacon on December 24, 1824. When they became engaged in 1824, they purchased a 250-acre parcel that bordered the Christiansville Quarter Horse Race Track, part of his grandfather William's estate. Reverend Adam Finch soon became a frequent speaker at the Christiansville Academy and the Concord Meetinghouse, where he met

Dr. John Draper, and he was one of the individuals who, along with his father, Zachariah, was responsible for establishing the Centenary Meetinghouse (circa 1840) in Christiansville. At some point, Finch started to be referred to as Dr. Finch, and this could be associated with his role at the academy. When the Christiansville Academy began, Dr. David Bigger was selected as the principal, and when he decided to retire, Reverend Finch became the new principal (which could have resulted in his being called "Dr.," following in the footsteps of Dr. Bigger). He became licensed as a minister in the county on November 19, 1849, and was responsible for performing many weddings through 1865. He was elected tax assessor of the Twenty-second Regiment on April 15, 1850. Later, his grandson Dr. Adam T. Finch inherited the farm, and the homeplace still stands, though in ruins.

The youngest surviving son of Adam and Mary Finch was Tyree Goode Finch, born on April 27, 1840. He had attended the academy, and when the war began, he was reportedly a student at Randolph Macon College. He left school and enlisted as a private in Company A, Third Virginia Cavalry, on May 14, 1861. He was not assigned to the company but was appointed as a field and services (F&S) quartermaster sergeant in charge of the commissary at Randolph Macon. There is documentation of his connection to the ordnance and commissary of Taylor's Ferry and the Clarksville Munitions and Ordinance Company.

Following the war, he became a respected planter, and in 1871, he was elected Mecklenburg County sheriff. He became a partner in the first tobacco warehouse (1871) in Boydton. He was also a principal in the newly established tobacco warehouse in Chase City (1873). He married his cousin Mary "Mollie" Jane Bacon Cunningham, widow of James Cunningham. Mollie (b. 1838) was the daughter of Colonel Lydall Bacon, whose land holdings were in Mecklenburg and Charlotte Counties. As a wedding gift, Mollie was given the Bacon plantation home with 497 acres of land, called "Ten Oaks." She and Tyree resided on the plantation for many years, and they had three daughters: Frances, Martha and Helen. They gave their son, Adam Tyree Finch (b. February 29, 1872), the plantation by deed around 1880. Ten Oaks burned in 1900. Subsequently, the farm was sold at least twice, and then it became known as the Roark Farm, located on present-day Black Branch Road (Highway 47), very near Black Branch Baptist Church. There is a Finch family cemetery on the farm.

Reverend Adam Finch took the school to a whole new level. With the aid of his wife, the school became coeducational soon after the fall term of 1835—something that existed nowhere else in Southside. In 1833, the

Virginia State Literary Fund was begun to assist academies in securing libraries and textbooks. The state allocated $80,000 for this purpose. For Mecklenburg County, the two delegates were gentry planter, overseer of the poor and justice Benjamin Whitehead Coleman and also Charles W. Baird. In 1834, as the state continued to fund this project, Richard Clausel Puryear (son of Samuel) replaced Baird and served for a number of years. With the success of the academy in Christiansville by 1838, it was considered a feeder school for Randolph Macon College in Boydton. But in 1858, Finch's wife died. He resigned from the academy and was replaced by John T. Brame, *Artium Baccalaureatus* degree, Randolph Macon College, class of 1839. On January 4, 1860, Reverend Finch married Martha W. Farrar.

From Elizabeth Pettus Puryear Pettus's "Letter to the Editor" in the *Chase City Progress* in 1888 and another in 1905, we know that she attended the Christiansville Academy, where Mr. E.T. Finch (who was the brother of Adam and the headmaster at the Clarksville Academy) brought in artists and painters from Baltimore and Richmond to instruct the students. He also brought in music instruction from Philadelphia. It appears the brothers shared resources.

Dr. Draper and May continued to lecture (both were sons of clergymen in England) there until the great epidemic of smallpox in 1835. Both May and Draper did what they could with their limited science. When the epidemic had passed, Dr. Draper left Christiansville and attended the Philadelphia Medical Institute. Draper completed his schooling there in 1836 and accepted a teaching position with Hampden-Sydney College in Prince Edward County, Virginia. There he taught for two years and began the Mineralogy Society and then accepted a position with the New York School of Medicine. He wrote one of the first textbooks on chemistry, published in New York in 1850.

May married Nancy Ann Simmons Smith (b. 1821), of Christiansville, on May 16, 1837, and they had two children: Charles E. (b. 1838) and John (b. 1840). In 1840, May left Christiansville and attended the Philadelphia Medical Institute, graduating in 1842. He returned to Christiansville to be with his family and then moved to Lunenburg County to establish his medical practice. Charles E. graduated from an academy in Lunenburg County and was working as a teacher before the war. During the Civil War, he was wounded in action twice but survived, and he returned home and married Martha Ann Stone Philips (widow of Samuel Phillips, who had died of a disease in the Confederate army), on November 1, 1865, and they had eight children. John died of yellow fever in 1861, while serving with the Confederate army in Texas.

On November 19, 1852, the circuit court of Mecklenburg County appointed Charles S. Hutcheson as superintendent of Mecklenburg County schools. A presiding justice of the circuit court and member of the board of trustees of Randolph Macon College, Hutcheson was born in 1804, lived near Boydton and was the son of John Ryland Hutcheson. His first wife was Elizabeth Wootton, who died during childbirth around 1845. Hutcheson served as superintendent for over ten years. At the close of the war, in memory of his son who had died of typhoid while serving in the Confederate army, he funded a scholarship program through Randolph Macon College.

THE WAR

A Principal Instrument of West African Tribes in the Fifteenth Century

The Banjar

Following the historical voyage of Christopher Columbus in 1492, the world, as it was previously known, changed dramatically. One of the first changes was trade, with never-before-seen merchandise from destinations that had not been charted before. Ships left Portugal, Spain, Turkey, Greece and Italy loaded with cargos of tea, spices, herbs, silk, fine linens, gold, silver and porcelain. First the ships would travel south to West Africa, where they would trade some of their wares for fresh food and slaves. The next stop would be South America—primarily Brazil—and fresh food, cotton, gold and gemstones were bartered. Traveling through the distant islands of the Lesser Antilles, especially Antigua and Barbuda, some of their cargo would be offloaded to begin some colonizing in the name of the ship captain's king or queen. As the years passed, by 1560, many ships began making the trip from Holland, England, France and Germany, and thus each island came under the rule of a different country (whoever conquered it next).

Generally, there was a skeleton crew of informal government, and most of the countries were interested in ownership with bragging rights but not in visiting or vacationing, like today. With little to do and no place to go or escape to, the slaves that were left to develop the islands preserved many of their African tribal customs—especially their music, which made up much of their waking life. The two primary musical instruments built and used by the slaves were the *toombah* (*tum tum*) an open-top shell drum that was generally struck with a stick of hardwood or a bone to create the music, and the *banjar*, which consisted of a wooden container with a flat top and bottom, attached to a reed-like stick. At the end of the stick, "gut" lines would be attached and drawn tightly to the center of the wooden container. The strings would be plucked or stroked to create the music. Both instruments were used outside for celebrations with dancing and partying. At one point in history, the islands that were owned by many of the European countries banned the African slaves from using the musical instruments. It was feared that the excitement of their performances was akin to pagan dances and "devil worship" ceremonies.

In an 1888 *Chase City Progress* article, Eliza Puryear wrote about visits to Christiansville and serenades by "Mr. Sweeney." In Southside Virginia, that name is probably one of the most famous in the world. Joel Walker Sweeney (1812–1860) was infatuated with the banjar, even as a very young child. Born and raised in nearby Appomattox, he spent many years with slaves in the neighborhood and local black musicians learning about the banjar. After all, if you were a real African musician, you knew how to build your own instruments.

Africans took pride in their musical skills and talents in building the instruments and performing with them. On September 5, 1983, the *News Progress* reprinted a story from the *Knoxville News-Sentinel* about a Clarksville-born slave, Pharaoh (Jackson) Chesney. It seems as though Pharaoh had gained a great degree of notoriety, "claiming" he had been born in Clarksville, Virginia, in 1785, and he said that on one occasion, he was with his master (Jonathan Jackson) and met George Washington. Jonathan's son Corban used to take Pharaoh on cattle buying trips, and on one such trip, they were in Tennessee. Corban liked the countryside so much that he began to purchase lands in Granger County in 1825. Soon after, Jonathan died, and in settling the estate, Corban sold Pharaoh for $421 in 1841 to John Chesney of Grainger County, Tennessee, who owned a very large milling operation in the area. Pharaoh built a cabin near the mill, and when the Civil War ended, he remained in his home. When interviewed (he was reportedly interviewed by many, including the writer of this particular article, Alex Haley) before he died in 1905, he was boastful of his life and certain of his age.

On July 5, 1882, an interview appeared in *Time* magazine. Aside from the history he remembered, he was very proud that he "knew how to make a banjo...not very hard. Almost any common mechanical genius could take an ordinary meal sieve hoop, fit a neck to it, stretch a raw cat hide across it, and put on some catgut strings." He was a colorful character in history, to say the least.

Joel Sweeney mastered building and playing the banjar, but soon it was called the banjo. His father was also a banjar "picker," but Joel is credited with adding a fifth string to the instrument and making it more popular. By 1840, the Sweeney Minstrels were touring throughout Virginia, Charleston, Baltimore, Philadelphia, Providence and New York. They became so popular that they received a special invitation from the queen of England, and they toured Great Britain from 1843 to 1845. In 1860, Joel died unexpectedly of dropsy. The Minstrels were on tour and performing in Washington, D.C. Soon after Joel's death, his eldest son, Richard Alexander, died.

Another son, Sampson "Sam" D. Sweeney, known as the "troubadour" or "banjo man," was also a virtuoso on the violin. When the Civil War began, he enlisted into Company H, Second Virginia Cavalry, as a private. In January 1862, he was reassigned to General J.E.B. Stuart as an entertainer. He died of smallpox at Orange Courthouse, Virginia, on January 13, 1864. One of his most famous songs was "Ole Joe Hooker," believed to have been written by Stuart.

This did not end the Minstrels. Joel's sister, Missouri, and his cousin Robert "Bob" continued to tour and perform. Bob's claim to fame was that

Trent Moody and his father, seven-time Grammy-nominated "Fiddlin'" Dwight Moody. Dwight Moody was also an accomplished banjo player. *Courtesy of the late Dwight Moody.*

The Philbeck Music House in Keysville, as seen in 2009. Banjo player Charlie Lankford (age ninety-three) is pictured with his brother, Hugh Lankford (age eighty-two), on the bass. *Courtesy of P. Hugh Lankford.*

he was left-handed. Another brother was Charles. When the war began, he also enlisted into Company H, Second Virginia Cavalry, as an "Appomattox Ranger." The following year, he transferred to Shoemaker's Company of Horse Artillery. Toward the close of the war, General Fitzhugh Lee arrived in Appomattox with his troops. On April 8, 1865, he used Charles Sweeney's home as his headquarters. The home is now listed on the National Register of Historic Places.

At least since the turn of the nineteenth century, the Piedmont Region has been home to many national, state and regional award-winning entertainers. One such person was the late Dwight Moody ("Mr. Fiddle Man"), who was equally skilled with a banjo and had received several Grammy awards. He and his family worked for almost fifty years with Disney Entertainment around the world, providing star-studded family musical entertainment. He began his career in the 1940s, playing wherever there was a platform, including the Grand Old Opry. Many of the musicians from the Piedmont began their performing at local music gatherings and in church.

Following World War II, more and more music houses began to open, hosting drop-in spots for musicians who wanted to practice with others and provide an entertainment program. Most people are familiar with the television show from the 1940s called *Grand Old Opry*. Obviously, the barn dance venue was used before the radio program, but that's where it gained in popularity, and then its popularity snowballed in the 1950s with Elvis Presley. The number of entertainers who've performed there could fill a volume by themselves.

One of the more popular local music houses that often hosts award-winning musicians from the state is the Philbeck House in Charlotte County, Keysville, Virginia. It was begun in the 1940s under the oak trees in the front yard at the home of the late Eddis Philbeck. It was later moved to the barn and then a small outbuilding, and now it is located in a large, modern, fully equipped music house owned and operated by Eddis's son, Larry Philbeck.

MEHERRIN FREE AND ACCEPTED MASONIC LODGE 119

The fourth son of William Tisdale, Richard Thomas Tisdale (May 30, 1837–March 10, 1902), was single and working on his father's farm when talk of the Civil War began. Richard, along with several others, felt the need for a strong Christian community with the impending war, and in the fall of 1860, they began to organize a Masonic Lodge. Tisdale was elected treasurer, and after the war, he held this position until his death.

The Meherrin Free and Accepted Masonic Lodge 186 was established, chartered and first met in December 1860 in the home of W.L. French, near Wayside (on the Finneywood–Charlotte County border.) The three officers elected in December were Samuel G. Johnson, Bartley C. Smithson and Robert S. Powell (Bartley C. and Samuel G. were neighbors, both were constables near Wightman and Samuel's son married Bartley's daughter). Richard was the treasurer. There was a membership of thirteen. In 1861, membership remained at thirteen, but because of the war, officers changed.

By way of background, Samuel Grigg Johnson (b. circa 1810) had served since 1852 as a justice of the peace for the Sixth District of Mecklenburg County, the Wightman area. Previously, he had served as a constable and part-time deputy sheriff beginning in 1843. Mecklenburg County seems to be a little different than most counties in Virginia. In Mecklenburg County, the justices of the peace served on the circuit court bench as gentlemen justices. Mecklenburg County justices appointed new justices every two years until about 1850, and then each district elected the justices, with the towns of Boydton and Clarksville also electing a justice, totaling sixteen. (South Hill wasn't recognized as a district until 1859.) In 1858–59, Johnson served during eleven court sessions and as acting presiding justice on several occasions.

The justices would meet in Boydton on the first court day in September of each year and elect one of their own to serve as the presiding circuit court judge. They would then divide into four seasonal groups, which would be assigned as their designated term to serve on the bench, presiding over court matters including both grand jury and petit jury cases. On May 20, 1861, one of fourteen justices present at court to vote for secession was Samuel G. Johnson.

Bartley Cox Smithson (b. 1813) was appointed the new superintendent of the poorhouse in Boydton, effective January 1, 1862. On May 19, 1862, the court instructed Smithson that he was responsible for securing the salt rations for the inmates of the poorhouse, once the salt shipment arrived in the county. If there were any surplus, he would be allowed to sell it for cash. In December 1862, he was appointed to a patrol for District 3 (Boydton). In April 1865, when Sheridan's troops occupied Boydton on their way to North Carolina, freedmen began to occupy vacant and government buildings in the town and other communities of the county. The freedmen took over the poorhouse complex and the buildings of the Randolph Macon College farm complex. The U.S. military troops condoned these occupations, and in May 1865, when Sherman's men came through Boydton, a company of soldiers was left to enforce martial law. The court was closed from April through August 1865, but when session was held in September 1865, one of the first items on the agenda was to approach the military adjutant and request the freedmen be removed from the poorhouse complex, and it was closed.

On December 22, 1883, at a special meeting of the board, Smithson was again appointed the superintendent of the poorhouse. Smithson had served several years as constable in Whittle's Mill area, Mecklenburg County. When he took over as superintendent of the poor, he was age seventy. Living with him on their farm at Whittle's Mill in 1880 was his son William (b. 1850), the farm manager, age thirty. His three daughters—Emma L. (Laura), age nineteen; Becky A., age fifteen; and Ada V., age thirteen—were at school. His other son, Edward B., was age six. His wife, S.C., was listed as age forty-seven. There was a house servant, Craddock Cephus, age fourteen, a black female.

On April 23, 1889, the board of supervisors appointed Smithson as a committee of one to negotiate with the A&D Railroad for the right of way through the poorhouse property. This he did. Smithson resigned in 1891 and died before 1897. The 1900 U.S. census records list S.C. Smithson (age sixty-seven, born March 1833, white, widow), with two of her daughters (A.B., born January 1868, and A.V., born July 1870). They were both working as schoolteachers. Living with the family was a servant, M. Crutchfield, white, female, born May 1870.

In 1866, former Confederate lieutenant Samuel "Ben" Johnson was appointed a captain in the Ninety-eighth Virginia Militia for the county. Among the freedmen, the military troops assigned here and carpetbaggers slithering into the county, the "demon rum" seemed to dictate much of the nightly and weekend behavior. There was a need for local citizens to assist with policing duties during Reconstruction. Johnson held this position until all the Virginia militias were ordered disbanded by U.S. Army general Stoneman, military leader of Virginia assigned to District 1 in Richmond in mid-1870.

In late 1867 or early 1868, the father, Samuel G., died and Ben Johnson (his son, b. 1841), was appointed administrator of the small estate. He was also the primary heir. He and his family lived out their lives in the Johnson neighborhood of Wightman, where he and his sons carried on the family tradition of success in business (operating the local country store) and government service (Ben served in the militia, and his son Robert served as the first postmaster of Wightman from January 1888 through 1900) and membership of the Masonic Lodge of Chase City (the new name for Christiansville in 1873).

Richard Tisdale enlisted in Company B, Thirty-fourth Virginia Infantry, in Christiansville on March 8, 1862, and was established at the rank of first sergeant. On May 13, 1863, he was promoted to lieutenant and then reported sick on July 23, 1863. He was wounded in the hand in May 1864 and was hospitalized in Richmond (reason unknown) on December 30, 1864.

On April 6, 1865, he was captured at Saylor's Creek and transported as a prisoner of war to "Old Capital Prison." On April 21, 1865, he was transferred to Johnson's Island. Many officers and sergeants were transferred to another facility and held captive for nearly three additional months following the assassination of President Lincoln. Tisdale was finally released on June 20, 1865, and sent home. He was described as five foot nine, with light hair and hazel eyes.

On December 16, 1883, at Concord Baptist Church, Richard married his third wife, Mamie A. Gregory (b. 1855), the elder sister of Lucius Gregory. In June 1890, they had one child, Mabry T. Tisdale. From 1888 through 1900, Richard served as one of the two elected overseers of the poor for the Christiansville District. On at least two occasions, he built or had made coffins for paupers. In 1880, Richard was a commissioner of revenue and tax appraiser for Chase City District and served in those positions until 1900. When the new Methodist church was built in Chase City in 1887, a Baptist layman came forward and presented the church with a new bell. That layman was Richard T. Tisdale.

Tisdale died on March 10, 1902, of a heart condition at the age of sixty-three. His will leaves provision for his daughter, Louisiana, and her four children. On May 19, 1926, Mamie Tisdale applied for a widow's pension, based on Richard's service. She was seventy-two and living with her son Mabry. She listed her assets as a house (that she did not live in) and a home (in which she did live), plus one-third interest in the store, with a value of $500, and she received $275 per year in interest.

On May 12, 1861, Robert S. Powell, age thirty-two, enlisted as a private in Company E, Fourteenth Virginia Infantry Regiment, in Clarksville. He listed his occupation as schoolteacher. He was described as light complexion, five foot eleven, with gray eyes and light hair. During September and October 1861, he was hospitalized for an unknown condition. He was given a Certificate of Disability Discharge on December 7, 1861, and sent home.

The new officers for 1861 were still Bartley C. Smithson, John J. Brown (who had no military service) and Richard Crenshaw. Crenshaw enlisted at the Stanton River Bridge into Company F, First Virginia Reserves (Farinholt's Division) and served guard until the war's end. Also, William A. Keeton enlisted in Company K, First Virginia Reserves (Farinholt's Division) on July 14, 1864. He was selected and established as a corporal. He enlisted at Mattoax, from Lunenburg County, and was described as a farmer, age forty-four. He also served guard for the duration of the war.

Members of the lodge were from around the county and some were from Charlotte and Lunenburg Counties. By 1888, they changed their meeting time from the second Saturday of each month to the Thursday "before a full moon" of each month. The meeting place for Lodge 186 was changed to the new Wightman post office in 1888, where they continued their meeting schedule of Thursday, with twenty-six members. B.C. Smithson was still active and served as the recording secretary. Richard T. Tisdale was the treasurer, and E.L. Baptist, from Baskerville, was the chaplain. Famous chair maker Warner Keeton Johnson, cousin of Samuel G., was also a member, as his farm and shop were only about one hundred yards from the meetinghouse.

In 1902, the Meherrin Masonic Lodge 186 became Chase City Masonic Lodge 119, with fifty members, located in one of the buildings that make up present-day Colgate's Square. By 1910, it had sixty-eight members. Next

Chase City Masonic Lodge 119 fraternal home has been located at Fourth and Boyd Streets since the 1950s. *Photo by Betty McKinney Caknipe.*

door, a new building was completed in 1912: Indian Motorcycle Sales and Service Center. If you drive south on Main Street in Chase City and come to Sycamore Street, look up, straight ahead above the Colgate's sign—the emblem still shines.

Around 1950, the Masonic lodge purchased a freestanding building, Jeffreys fertilizer storehouse, at the corner of Fourth and Boyd Streets. The Masons relocated and still call that building home.

THE MILITIA IS FORMED

J ohn Brown was reported to be recruiting in Mecklenburg County in the summer of 1859. He reportedly visited the plantations of Mark Anthony, Henry Coleman, William Towns and John Nelson, all along the Roanoke River. Several years later, a Mrs. Mary E. Pleasants wrote that in fact, it was she, dressed like a jockey, who visited the plantations, accompanied by a male companion. She was from Canada and a strong supporter of Brown's mission.

Until this time, Mecklenburg County had been in its glory. Ideally located on the river, Clarksville boasted a large tobacco market and the Roanoke Navigation Company (bateaux shipping and a river port), which was begun in 1820 by William Birchette, president, and David Shelton, treasurer, and extended to Clarksville before 1830. There were two banks and a wagon factory, and with a population of over one thousand people, it was the largest town in the county. In 1856, a railroad spur from Weldon, North Carolina, came to Clarksville, which now with a population of two thousand. The spur added a passenger service and a greater shipping operation from towns upstream (Danville, South Boston and Brookneal) and brought many tourists to the Buffalo Springs Resort.

Boydton was the second-largest town, with nearly five hundred people, plus the thriving Randolph Macon College, with over three hundred people. It was followed by St. Tammany, a river port community of three hundred people, and Christiansville with slightly less. The best tobacco and cotton markets ever were in the 1850s, coupled with a continuous demand for pedigree horses and

The Dan and Roanoke Rivers converge at Clarksville (Fort Occoneechee). Occoneechee Island is the center ground in this 1927 photograph. *Courtesy U.S. Army, Corps of Engineers.*

a steady market of slaves. Alas, the town's affluence was all coming to an end. As many as half of the plantation children were already moving west to find a new, simpler, small-farming lifestyle. The horse market had been replaced by the new breeders in Tennessee, and Kentucky was gaining ground. The Meherrin River bridge collapsed, and toll roads from Boydton to Petersburg and Clarksville to Oxford Plank were in serious disrepair. The former was closed and sold at auction in 1861. The Roanoke Valley Railroad extension through Clarksville was a year behind schedule in 1856 and would soon be scrapped for the war effort. Soon, emotional energies turned to a new target, with a vengeance: the politicians of the North.

John Brown's raids and reputation were a wake-up call to the United States, and especially to the South, that troubled times were coming. Lee and Stuart were ordered from Washington, D.C., with U.S. Marine troops to defend Harper's Ferry, yet John Brown was never charged with a federal crime, even though he raided a federal arsenal and killed a U.S. Marine. The federal government was mute. In the North, he was being martyred by clergy and media. *Harper's Weekly* carried a story stating that his only crime was against "Aristocratic Virginia."

Another blow came to Mecklenburg County, when U.S. congressman William O. Goode, representing the southern Virginia district and residing in Boydton, died in 1859 at the age of fifty-nine. Selected to fill out his term was his nephew, a commonwealth's attorney and son of Dr. Thomas Goode. Thomas F. Goode Jr. was already talking of secession. He was the keynote speaker on November 21, 1859, in Boydton and again on November 26, 1859, in Clarksville, encouraging secession in light of Lincoln potentially being elected president.

Goode pointed out that, the "North will invade us." There were 16,000 federal troops serving in the United States. Of this number, 800 were out west, fighting the Indians, while 1,700 guarded Washington, D.C., and the North, but in the South, there were 13,500. The North was already here, just waiting for orders to move. Of note is the 1860 U.S. census records, which list Mecklenburg County, Virginia, as having 20,096 citizens. Of these, were 6,777 whites, 900 free blacks and 12,419 slaves.

The day after Virginia citizens voted to secede from the United States on May 21, 1861, at a court session in Boydton, a slave, Sam, property of John H. Winckler, was charged that "he did plot and conspire to rebel, and make insurrection." The circuit court appointed an attorney, former justice and professor of the Law Department at Randolph Macon College Edward R. Chambers, to represent him. He was found guilty by unanimous decision of the petit jury and judges and ordered sent to jail until such time as the sheriff could transport him to Richmond to be sold to a buyer who would take him out of the United States. The judges deliberated his cost, with two appraising him at $500 and one at $600. They paid Winckler $540 in settlement.

The militia was formed in Mecklenburg County before 1765 by the king of England to protect the settlers and to be prepared for attacks by invading forces. When Mecklenburg County was formed in 1765, there were two militia units in place: the Twenty-second and Ninety-eighth Virginia Militia Regiments of the Fifteenth Battalion, First Division, with one responsible for coming to the aid from the east to the coast and the other to aid from the west to the mountains. It was a mandatory service and consisted of training one weekend each month. After the Revolutionary War, the militia continued, of necessity, and seemed to follow in the footsteps of their counterparts from New England. In New England, for over one hundred years before the Revolutionary War, it was law that a tavern must be located about every eight miles along highways and there must be sufficient taverns in each town or community to meet the needs of the citizens.

The taverns provided some form of nourishment and a local destination for community and business meetings. It was a familiar location to the local people and was also the location used to store the armaments for the militia. That was only logical, as the militia met at the tavern before training and returned there to store their weapons and to partake of a beverage or two over some conversation. The local militia units were called to duty between 1812 and 1814 during the War of 1812. There is documentation that Captain Samuel F. Bugg turned in his weapons (retiring) to Captain William Baskervill, of the Ninety-eighth Regiment, at Lombardy Grove Tavern on May 12, 1836, just before the Trail of Tears campaign in western North Carolina began in 1837.

The justices of the county, being mindful of the political fervor in the United States, sought to take early action to defend the county. At court day on April 19, 1858, according to the Circuit Court Record of April 19, 1858, "The court doth appoint James T. Alexander, John J. Brown, and John T. Williams, commissioners, to oversee elections for the Ninety-eighth Regiment; elections, at a place, and time they appoint, to elect regimental, and company officers. Also, the court doth appoint William A. Blanch, George J. Dabbs, and E. J. Goode, commissioners, to oversee elections for the Twenty-second Regiment; elections, at a place, and time they appoint, to elect regimental, and company officers." Generally, elections were held at the community taverns.

In Boydton, the Boyd Tavern served as the local militia meeting place, and it is conceivable that the cellar was used not only to store the fine imported liquors but also the armaments for a large militia detail of men. Puryears Tavern in Christiansville, Lombardy Grove Tavern for the Flat Creek community, the William Jones Storehouse for the St. Tammany community, Tanner's Store for the Poplar Springs and Blackridge communities, Royster's Tavern in Clarksville and Buffalo Springs Tavern served as the countywide meeting, polling and probable militia storage places. That is also part of the explanation as to why some of these locations were so prominent during the recruitment of militia volunteers for service in the Civil War.

On November 21, 1859, at the county meeting in Boydton, the citizens concluded that Southerners, "as a prudent people," should "look alone to our resources for the protection of our property and our lives, against the incursions of our enemies." The South was now a self-contained entity. At the follow-up meeting in Clarksville on November 26, 1859, a resolution was passed "that we deeply and sincerely deplore any trains of events calculated to impair the permanency of the union, nevertheless, we are ready to yield it up with all its prestige and glorious recollections, when circumstances constrain us to look to its dissolution as one of the chief means of securing safety for ourselves, our families and our property."

Also, the citizens wanted the county to offer its services to Governor Wise, should he need them. It was further recommended that an additional two or more "efficient volunteer military companies in the County of Mecklenburg" be organized. Another meeting was scheduled to be held in Clarksville in February 1860. Military activity in the county came alive in 1860. On May 10, 1860, couriers delivered invitations to many of the county men for a "Pic-Nic," to be held in Boydton on June 14, 1860, as a retirement party for Colonel John R. Chambless Jr., most likely, on the grounds of the college. This was being hosted by E.R. Chambers, president (also a judge and law professor at Randolph Macon College); Dr. William H. Jones, vice-president (MD and owner of the drugstore in Boydton); John M. Tucker, vice-president (owner of over three thousand acres); R.P. Alexander, vice-present (co-owner of the drugstore); O.H.P. Corprew, vice-president (professor at R.M. College); Captain Alexander Sydnor, vice-president (veteran of the War of 1812, owner of Washington Tavern and manager of Bruce's Mercantile); B.R. Williamson, vice-president (justice); and Thomas L. Jones, vice-president (owner of the Boydton Tanning Yard). The businessmen of the county were thoroughly convinced that Virginia was going to be invaded by a Northern insurrection or even that an all-out war would occur.

Those Lunenburg County men were "all fired up." Right after the attack on Harpers Ferry, they met in 1859 and began recruiting for the "Lunenburg Light Dragoons" all in the same day. The company was commanded by Captain William E. Stockdell. They began training the new recruits, and the county was already talking about secession. (The Light Dragons went on to become Company G, Ninth Virginia Cavalry—"Lee's Rangers"—under the command of Captain W.H. Fitzhugh Lee.) There were some eager Mecklenburg County boys who joined as well.

Mecklenburg County responded quickly following the meetings. In December, the Boydton Cavalry, "Mecklenburg Dragoons," part of the Boydton militia, organized and even ordered uniforms. This became Company A, Third Virginia Cavalry. There is also documentation of a State Line Militia/Cavalry, which remained for county defense. Part of the militia became an infantry unit, and one squad—First Division, Second squad—was the Butchers Creek militia. The squad leader was Sergeant John W. Wootton, Esq., and the squad consisted of J.J. Wootton, Joseph Wootton, Edward

Overton, J.T. Carter, J.H. Wootton, A.F. Davidson, D.A. Carter, Richard Jeffress, James H. Jerrereys, A.K. Atkins and J.R. Stuart.

Other units were being organized at the same time. In Clarksville, the organizers were L.E. Finch and J.G. Sneed, forming the Roanoke Guard (neither individual served in the military). During the war, they were involved in operating the local commissary of the CSA. They were county commissioners as well. In Sandy Fork, it was Captain R. Camillus Overby, whose unit became Company G (Third), Fifty-ninth Regiment of Virginia Volunteers, but upon arrival in Richmond, they were reassigned to become Company C, Second Battalion, North Carolina Infantry. Overby had enlisted on May 14, 1861, as a private in Company A, Third Virginia Cavalry. He transferred to Company G of the Fifty-ninth when they offered him the position of captain.

As part of their ongoing training, the militia units maintained constant patrols of the county's countryside and towns, especially during the late fall and winter (spring and summer were for planting and harvesting). While on patrol, of course, they got in some target practice and brought home food for the table. By the fall of 1860, the county recognized the militia units for serving as special police units. They were in communities, serving guard duty during the evenings, and they assisted with guarding special events, as well as became noted political figures. They were also required to be on the watch for any signs of insurrection by the slaves or free blacks. The year 1860 was a very busy one, but most importantly of all the events of that year were the political races—especially the presidential race, with seven leading candidates and regional candidates totaling eleven political parties.

By best estimate, Mecklenburg County consisted of almost 1,400 households in 1860, with over half of the population being female. Of course, the first question posed is often: how many men were killed? For the Veterans' War Memorial in Clarksville, CW-3 chief warrant officer, third grade (ret.) Ron A. Bugg, et al, had found 353 names of Civil War soldiers that died during the war. But with this story, the number identified has risen to 416, and there will be more. The total of 416 is debated by some historians as the 416th soldier would be Robert Richardson. It appears from a brief newspaper obituary that Robert moved to Boydton in 1860 from Danville and was working for the county. With the fervor of the recruitment activity in Boydton, it appears that Robert enlisted into Captain Townes Jr.'s company of "Mecklenburg Rifles" on or before May 30, 1861. He was found dead at the age of nineteen in his room on May 31, 1861, when he did not report for work. The editor of the *Tobacco Plant* added a note: "This needs to be reprinted in Danville."

ROBERT H. MASON

THE ONLY SOUTHSIDE FATALITY AT THE BATTLE OF STANTON RIVER BRIDGE

It seems that in any given year between 1790 through 1870, there were at least eighty-five Puryears in Mecklenburg County, many with the same first name. In researching Elizabeth Puryear's youngest sister, (Martha) Virginia Puryear (b. August 27, 1842), I had arrived at a wonderful story—but one more resource proved that the whole story was actually about her cousin.

Virginia (Jennie) H. Puryear was born in January 1841 in Clarksville. Her parents were William Marshall Puryear (1810–1888) and Louisa J. Tarwater (1814–1890s), the daughter of Michael Tarwater (one of the wealthiest men in Clarksville from 1820 through the 1840s; he was a horse racing enthusiast and owner of Thoroughbreds and two studs). William was the son of Thomas Puryear (1785–1838) and Elizabeth Goode Marshall (1790–1852), who were married on May 23, 1805, in Clarksville. (Now, for the genealogists, Peter Jefferson married Jane Randolph in 1738, and they begot Thomas Jefferson II. He became author of the Declaration of Independence and third president of the United States in 1801. They also begot Lucy Goode Jefferson, who married Colonel William Marshall, brother of Chief Justice John Marshall, and they begot Elizabeth Goode Marshall.)

William became an accomplished saddler and worked in that profession for many years. In the 1860 census, he was listed as being worth $3,500 in land and $7,688 in personal property. He and Louisa had five children: Betty Catherine (b. 1835), Robert (b. 1838), Virginia (b. 1841), Benjamin (b. 1844) and Hanna (b. February 1850). During the Civil War, the saddle shop was taken over by the Confederate army in the fall of 1862. A new

SOUTHSIDE VIRGINIA CHRONICLES

blacksmith was added to the factory: Charles Russell, from Washington City. Fearful that the Richmond saddle, tack and munitions factory would be taken by Union forces, the Confederate army sent Russell to Clarksville (the closest factory to the supply of cattle hides) to expand it for other munitions, including wagons.

Former apprentices of Puryear were Benjamin F. Puryear (his son) and Robert H. Mason. Robert H. Mason enlisted in Company A, Third Virginia Cavalry, at Boydton on May 14, 1861, and was established at the rank of sergeant. On August 18, 1862, he was discharged from Confederate service to better use his skills for the war effort as a saddler. With his return to Clarksville on March 19, 1863, Mason married William's daughter, Virginia. With the long arduous hours in the factory, there was no time for a honeymoon, much less time off.

In June 1864, the alarm was sounded in Southside that Union troops were moving along the rail lines, destroying and looting as they moved, with a destination of the Stanton River Bridge in Charlotte County. That bridge was key to a major Southern supply route to Confederate troops. The munitions factory closed and every able-bodied man (and probably children and many wives) loaded onto bateaux and headed upstream to the bridge. Having made a hasty preparation for battle, Union forces arrived late in the morning on June 25, 1864, and began an artillery attack. Seeing that the Southerners were not intimidated, they initiated a frontal assault but were repelled twice. Then, under the cover of darkness, they retreated.

Charles Russell had been shot in the head but recovered. William Puryear was not injured, and on January 20, 1865, he enlisted in Company C, First Virginia Reserves, and stood guard on the bridge until the war's end. He had enlisted to be with his son. Benjamin F. enlisted in the First Virginia Reserves, Company A, in Clarksville on April 22, 1864. He fought at the battle of Stanton River Bridge, staying on to guard the bridge. Sick with scabies, he was hospitalized at Farmville Hospital from November 22 to December 10, 1864, and returned to duty on December 31, 1864. He died three days after his father joined him at the bridge on January 23, 1865.

In the fall of 1863, the South was still convinced that it would prevail over the North. A textbook publisher in Raleigh, North Carolina, published an elementary school math book titled *Johnson's Elementary Arithmetic*. These are some of the study questions:

- A Confederate soldier captures 8 Yankees each day for 9 successive days, how many did he capture in all?

- If one Confederate soldier kills 90 Yankees how many Yankees will 10 Confederate soldiers kill?
- If one Confederate soldier can whip 7 Yankees, how many soldiers can whip 49 Yankees?

A synopsis of Mecklenburg County's involvement in the war includes over fourteen companies of men who were volunteers from Mecklenburg County throughout the war, as well as many county citizens who enlisted into units formed in Lunenburg, Halifax and Charlotte Counties of Virginia and Warren, Vance and Granville Counties, North Carolina. Throughout the war, soldiers sought out and joined companies they wanted to belong to. Seventeen Mecklenburg County officers were at the surrender with Lee at Appomattox. Eight Mecklenburg County companies were at Gettysburg and participated in Picket's Charge.

More than 1,400 men served, which was over 70 percent of all white males in the county of age during that time frame. Some volunteers on the battlefield were as young as eleven, and over 400 died while fighting for Mecklenburg County. The family in the county with the most sons serving and dying was the Puryears (twenty-four and thirteen, respectively). Another family, the Newtons, had twenty-three serving.

On January 28, 1920, Virginia Puryear Mason Geoghegan applied for a widow's pension, based on her first husband's death at the bridge. Before the battle at the bridge, all volunteers were sworn in as CSA Army, but her application was rejected on July 12, 1920, as the War Department found no record of her husband's service. In defense of her application, she submitted a sworn affidavit on July 18, 1920, that stated, "I, J.W. Rhodes...found the said Robert F. Mason dead, at the foot of said Stanton River Bridge, with a gunshot, or rifle ball wound in his body; that I personally assisted in placing him in a river bateau for the purpose of sending his remains to Clarksville." Mason was the only fatality from Southside at the Battle of Stanton River Bridge. Virginia did eventually receive her pension of thirty dollars per year.

RECONSTRUCTION

POST-CIVIL WAR

CHRISTIANSVILLE ACADEMY

During the war, the school continued to operate. Then Pettus (died 1864) and Keene used the building to sign-up volunteers for the military (primarily the Twenty-first Virginia Infantry and First Virginia Reserves). Dignitaries continued to visit and lecture but a lot less frequently than before the war. In 1867, the school was beginning to rebound from the devastation of the war, but John T. Brame had sold his farm and was going to move to Missouri. He resigned from the academy and was replaced by Reverend J.L. (M.) Kirkpatrick. It appears that Kirkpatrick may have been a graduate of Randolph Macon College in Boydton, receiving one of the first bachelor of English language and science degrees in 1854. This was a new degree from RMC that year and did not require the classics, so Kirkpatrick taught, preached and prayed in English—not Latin, as the practice was in the day. Graduation exercises were now conducted in English rather than Latin also.

On July 4, 1869, the Christiansville Presbyterian Church was established, with George Endly having been elected as the ruling elder. The records of the church also state, "Rev. John M. Kirkpatrick entered upon his labors as a stated supply on the first Sabbath in September 1869. On the first Sabbath in October 1869 the sacrament of the Lords supper was administered in this church and Mrs. A.W. Kirkpatrick, and Miss Ruth Kirkpatrick were received on certificate from the Danville Church."

To bolster enrollment, advertisements began to appear in the *Tobacco Plant*, a Clarksville newspaper distributed throughout the county, in 1869 and

Chase City Presbyterian Church is seen in the background during this 1963 fair parade, featuring the Bluestone High School marching band in the foreground. *Photo from author's collection.*

continued for the next two years (paid for by George Endly and John Boyd, who were now on the board of directors of the school). The ads read:

> *The course of instruction will embrace all the branches usually taught in a first class school. Terms of tuition (per session of ten months) will be as follows:*
> *For pupils in primary departments, embracing Reading, Writing and the first four rules of*
> *Arithmetic*   *$30.00*
> *For the higher branches of English and the elements of Algebra 40.00*
> *For the Classics and higher Mathematics*   *50.00*
> *For music on the piano, two lessons per week*   *30.00*
> *For use of the Instrument*   *5.00*
> *For French, extra*   *15.00*
> *Tuition will be payable quarterly in advance.*

A recess of ten days will be given at Christmas, and the last session will close on the last Friday in June.

The religious preferences of the pupils will not be interfered with and all sectarian influence will be carefully avoided, but the School will be opened each day with reading the Scriptures and prayer.

During the Christmas break in 1869, a two-day celebration was held by the community for support of the school. On December 22, 1869, according to an editorial in the January 5, 1870 *Tobacco Plant*:

Some sixty ladies and gentlemen assembled at the residence of Rev. J.M. Kirkpatrick, in the village of Christiansville, bringing with them a variety of useful domestic articles as corn, flour, pork, fowls, vegetables, cream, etc., a large supply of cakes, domestic wine and other delicacies, and also several handsome presents of clothing as a Christmas donation to the Reverend and his family.

It may be proper to state that the party included members of different denominations residing in and around Christiansville who thus generously contributed to inaugurate the festivities of the season by an expression of their good will, both suitable and timely.

But it didn't stop there. A letter was sent to the editor as a follow-up and published in the same edition of the paper. Apparently, the next night was for a party with the Endlys, but the letter explains what happened.

On Thursday, December 23rd, at Christiansville, [local citizens] *might be seen hurrying to and fro, coming from every direction, and congregating at Mr. Endly's house.* [As an aside, he had just lost his wife in the spring.]

After much talking and planning, we form a line and march, double file, to the residence of Rev. J.M. Kirkpatrick. What means this marching in file? What this confusion? What the squalling of old hens, the quacking of ducks, these blankets and bundles? What is up? Now we reach the house. In we march, two by two, without ceremony. They coming bearing, now a basket, now a bundle, then a toy for the little ones, now a dress, then a basket of apples—now J.P.R. and W.H. come with measured step and slow, bearing a table laden with a good old Virginia ham, surrounded by six good old Virginia cabbages, (Bacon and Greens), and a fat old hen (chicken pie), Jerry brings up the rear, exclaiming, hurry up, look out, let me come, and rolling a barrel of flour.

Baptists, Methodists and Episcopalians join in their contributions, and the hearts of the beloved Pastor and family are made glad. We are soon invited to partake of a bountiful supper. Then we spend an hour or two in amusing games and social converse. Time glides swiftly away, and ere we are aware of it, the evening has passed. We go to our homes, feeling that we have been engaged in a good work. It will be long before those pleasant hours are forgotten.

In 1870, Kirkpatrick was sent by the M.E. Conference of Virginia to the Baltimore conference to establish a relationship and to raise $80,000 for an endowment fund to replace what Randolph Macon College (now in Ashland) had lost due to the war. He appears to have been quite successful in his efforts. It seems that he was appointed to the RMC board of trustees. Replacing him as principal of the academy was Tingal Brame, a member of the Methodist Episcopal Church, South, North Carolina Conference. At the same time, Brame's brother, James H. Brame, became principal of the Boydton Male Academy. In 1873, Brame was responsible for having the name changed to the Chase City Academy, but also in 1873, the carpetbaggers began to arrive in town. Brame was ably assisted in his instructions by Dr. Thomas Drew, the new Presbyterian reverend, as well as his son, Allen, and daughter, Hortense. When Brame left in 1875–76, somehow the United Presbyterian Church of North America (the local carpetbaggers), took it over for the education of the "new arrivals" from Ohio and Pennsylvania.

Reverend John Y. Ashenhurst served as a pastor in Hayesville, Ohio, and arrived in Mecklenburg County in 1870, soon followed by eight more families. Ashenhurst immediately began to attempt to "hoodwink" farmers into selling him land "in the name of the Church." He was successful, and in 1875, he wrote to the Presbyterian Board that he had secured $100,000 in property on behalf of the church (though what he did with the money—or was it property in his name?—is unknown). He wrote his son John J., who owned a newspaper in Ohio, and John J., in turn, published the letter in his paper. The son either sent or brought copies of the newspaper when he came to Chase City for a visit and passed them around town. The July 1873 letter states, in part: "Today Virginia is suffering more by selfish acts of political Adventurers from the North than any internal disease."

On the heels of this paper, John Y. became the new Town of Chase City developer and George Endly's greatest nemesis. Ashenhurst immediately organized the new arrivals into a protest against the Christiansville Presbyterian Church, South, saying, in a nutshell, "That ain't the way we do it up North." They built their own church less than a block away, the United Presbyterian Church of North America, and withdrew support from the existing Christiansville Church. Of these families, whose names do not deserve to be written here, none built businesses, and only two or three built small four-room homes. They didn't last long, as they quickly sold out, took their profits and moved west. All of the families that followed Ashenhurst were gone in five years.

When Ashenhurst's son arrived in town, he could immediately see the potential. But he quickly returned to Ohio. After all, he was running for governor (northern politician—carpetbagger!). He lost the election to his opponent, William McKinley, returned to Christiansville and brought with him printing equipment and supplies. In the spring of 1874, the *Chase City Enterprise* was begun (although I have found no copies or microfilm copies). John J., the son, was a newspaperman, not a teacher. He was a lay elder in the church but not a preacher. During the war, he was an artificer for the Fourteenth Ohio Artillery, and he came to the new Chase City for one thing: money. In 1875–76, Reverend John took over the Chase City Academy and appointed his son the new principal.

Reverend John was aware that the Mission Board in Pennsylvania, by its arrangement with the U.S. adjutant general's office, wanted to establish a school in Chase City. In 1876, with his church failing and his congregation all but gone, Reverend Ashenhurst wrote to the Board of Missions. He stated that due to his ill health, he was returning to Ohio (although he did not leave until 1878, following the opening of the school, and he lived until 1892), but he was leaving his son in charge of his holdings to dispose of the same. He also referenced that his son was a principal and teacher at the local academy and would do well in the new school—Thyne Institute.

After an extended period of time (several months), the Mission Board offered the position to John J. He accepted the appointment and immediately began preparations for the new school. In late 1876, and early 1877, he sold the newspaper and closed the Chase City Academy (the new arrivals had left town and his efforts to consolidate it with the new Presbyterian black school were met with naught) in preparation for his appointment. He spent much of his time with real estate transactions until the school opened in the fall of 1878. He left Chase City in 1880, having finally sold most of his and his father's speculations for a sizable profit. He returned to the newspaper business in Ohio. He later wrote a book about his father, Reverend John Y., and how he had come to Chase City and saved the town and county from "Satan himself—who had been standing at the door." The Presbyterian Church of North America was sold to the Baptists and, in 1876, became the Chase City Baptist Church.

BUILDING OF FAIRVIEW AND THYNE INSTITUTE

Near the old Burwell schoolhouse, a new settler purchased a farm. William H. Dunlap arrived in Christiansville in March 1872. He had been a building contractor in Pennsylvania (he did not serve in the Union army) with his son even before the Civil War. After the war, he was appointed by the Presbyterian Mission Board, to come to Christiansville (apparently, the board had been notified by Endly about the developing community) to build and establish a Freedmen's Bureau. Dunlap purchased a 172-acre farm on Lunenburg Courthouse and Black Branch Roads with 102 acres south of Black Branch and 102 acres north. That same month, he sold the 70-acre parcel south of the road to the Mission Board for a freedman's bureau for $686.40 and began to build the schoolhouse. He retained the 102 acres north of the road, which also contained a small home. He remodeled and expanded the home for his family and boarders. In 1902, it became a boardinghouse.

Because of his position, he was immediately appointed to the Southside Board of Settlers and was one of the representatives who accompanied Boyd and Endly to Richmond to meet with Salmon P. Chase. The Freedman's Bureau and Board of Settlers were similar in that they were for the "protection, cooperation and concentration of opinions and experiences" of their membership. The Freedman's Bureau also had the responsibility of teaching reading, writing, arithmetic, home economics, farming and independent living to the black community.

Dunlap and family joined the Christiansville Presbyterian Church in April 1872. Restoring and remodeling the farmhouse in which his family lived, Dunlap

The William Dunlap home in Fairview was remodeled in 1870, likely using some of the first prefabricated products from the shop of Jacob Holt. *Courtesy of the late Faye McKinney.*

and Son (James) became the contractors of the new Chase City. They built their first home in June 1873. The Honorable John Huston (also of Pennsylvania and a member of the same church) contracted to build a "fine residence and business" (drugstore) at the southeast corner of Fifth (Barnesville Road) and Main Streets, followed by the residence of William D. Patterson (of the same church) at the southwest corner, then the Presbyterian manse (parsonage) at the northwest corner and the Jackson Hotel at the northeast corner. He built the homes of most all of the new members of the Presbyterian church. In the summer of 1874, several new settlers arrived from Dunlap's area of Pennsylvania.

They proved to be instigators and carpetbaggers but persuasive. The Presbyterian church was divided, and a new one built less than a block away. The group had been led by Reverend R.H. King, but as soon as the building of the new church was begun by Dunlap, he left town along with five other dissenters. Then in 1876, a new member came to town—John Thyne. It appears that he lived for a while with the Dunlap family and worked at the Dunlap and Son sawmill.

John Thyne (b. 1843) had been a clerk at a bookstore in New York City. Receiving the inheritance from his mother's estate, he apparently came to Southside after seeing the advertisements. Working for Dunlap and attending church with the Dunlap family at the new Presbyterian Church of North America, he met Reverend Ashenhurst, who had purchased land next to the Freedman's Bureau property. Thyne purchased a five-acre parcel in the fall of 1876 from Ashenhurst directly across the road from Dunlap's sawmill and built himself a home.

In March 1877, Thyne sent a deed for the property to the Presbyterian Mission Board with a stipulation that he would give the board his property and home and would build a schoolhouse if it would purchase the materials. The board agreed, and Wilson Hall was completed in 1876. With the completion of the hall and the Presbyterian Church of North America already sold, Thyne left town (not having paid for the property).

In 1881, Dunlap's daughter Ada died. Dunlap and family returned to the Chase City Presbyterian Church that same year. Also in 1881, the new principal for Thyne Elementary School was Reverend Dr. John Veazy, a former Federal army officer who had served during Reconstruction. With seventy-five acres of property, Veazy saw the opportunity for a community, which he called "Fairview." He launched a campaign, with the help of Dunlap, which resulted in new homes for area families and Wilson Hall, Thyne's home and the Freedman's Bureau all being enlarged to better accommodate both students and faculty.

In 1883, the railroad arrived. This was "boom time" for Fairview and Chase City. With Dunlap's saw- and lumber mill next to the tracks in Fairview, he was in a perfect location for the explosion of building over the next five years. Then in 1888, his youngest son, Hervey, died at the age of thirty-four. During his twenty-four years in Chase City, Dunlap and Son built over fifty homes, two school complexes, at least one church and several businesses (though no brick structures that I could find), leaving quite a legacy. There is some stir in the area as to what Dunlap built and remodeled versus what the legendary Jacob Holt and his son William built and remodeled. In either case, Holt is considered the "father" of prefabricated building. His lumber yard and building warehouse was only one mile south by the rail line, and it would seem only logical that with the volume of work Dunlap completed, he must have relied on prefabricated products from Holt.

From the design of the buildings, it appears he built the Southside Military Institute in 1891. But perhaps his last building was that of the boys' dormitory for the new Thyne Institute, completed in 1893 (he would have been sixty-seven at the time). He died in his home on June 14, 1896, at the age of seventy. He is buried in the Dunlap plot of the Woodland Cemetery. After his burial, his wife and two remaining children returned to her family in Pennsylvania.

On July 30, 1898, the Bank of Chase City foreclosed on the home and the 102 acres. In 1899, the property was sold to a new arrival from North Carolina: J.L. Woodyard and family. With the migration of farmers to the area from North Carolina and the building of the Mecklenburg Mineral Springs Hotel/Sanitarium, Woodyard did not want to pay the boardinghouse fee and taxes. His family lived in the home, but when a new arrival came to town from North Carolina to build in the community, he would simply sell his home to him. Once the recent arrival's home and business/farm was established, Woodyard would buy his own home back, less the rental charge. The first such family was that of Robert S. McCall, followed by J.C. Collis and others.

Reverend Henry G. McGonegal

Northern Baptist Missionaries in Southside

William Dunlap had been sent to what was to become the new town of Chase City, arriving in late 1870 to investigate the feasibility of establishing a United Presbyterian community. It appears that he was also to establish a new Freedmen's Bureau on behalf of the United Presbyterian Missions Board of Pittsburgh. This was done in short order, but then the carpetbaggers began to arrive. Dunlap and family were not alone when they arrived in Christiansville, but they were some of the earliest Presbyterians. Many good men arrived in the county over the next eight years, with many settling in Chase City and even more in Boydton.

George Endly and other Presbyterians arrived from western Pennsylvania in the late summer and early fall of 1868 and began the development of a new community. The Baptists arrived in the fall of 1869, with one being from south central New York, representing the American Baptist Home Mission Board, which was also under contract with the U.S. adjutant general's office. Two of the most notable of the Baptists were elder Reverend Daniel Fowler Leach (June 27, 1817–September 10, 1889), from the American Baptist Home Mission Board, and the second was little-known Reverend Henry G. McGonegal (also spelled McGonagall), D.D. (d. 1875) from the Home Mission Board in Connecticut. Arriving in Christiansville, Reverend Leach purchased property and settled in for the long haul.

Reverend McGonegal (a younger man), on the other hand, saw the old vacant Randolph Macon College campus, and he proceeded to develop local support and finances to begin a new college in the county. Much was written about him in 1871 and 1872 in the Roanoke Valley newspaper. But that's about as clear as his story gets. However, it is clear that these two men, McGonegal and Leach, were acquainted with each other, as both men were involved with the Concord Baptist Association and were in the Concord Baptist Church community at the same time.

According to the newspapers, in 1871, Dr. McGonegal, having secured the backing of the Concord Baptist Association, was establishing the South Side Seminary. The first semester was slated to begin on October 1, 1871. McGonegal purchased the primary Randolph Macon College buildings and six parcels of the property on February 15, 1871, according to the deeds in Boydton. The purchase price of $12,500 was financed through a note, held by John Howard of Richmond. It was advertised as a "first class male school," headed by Professor J.W. Jones in the R.M. College Building. (Jones was Captain John W. Jones, previously the headmaster of Zion Academy in Union Level, Virginia. He was also a graduate of Randolph Macon College, A.B., 1859). The first semester opened with twenty-five students, and the newspaper covered the story of the "South Side Seminary College" opening in its November 4, 1871 issue.

Another story in the paper on November 4 was about the first ministers and deacons meeting of the Concord Baptist Association at Concord Church "on Friday, Saturday and Sunday, October 27th, 28th, and 29th'" (1871). Due to bad weather, only five ministers were present on Friday, and one of those was McGonegal (throughout the story he is referred to as R. McGonegal). On Sunday, "in the afternoon Rev. R. McGonegal preached from Luke, 5th Chapter, 10th verse. The sermon was eloquent and beautiful." During the noon hour, two deacons had been ordained, with Reverend R. McGonegal, D.D., "giving the charge."

Prior to the close of the meeting a resolution was offered by Major W.S. Downer:

> *Whereas, to view of the importance to our land of the education of youth, and their training in the ways of truth and righteousness; and of the fact that the buildings, formerly of Randolph Macon College have passed into the hands of a minister of the Baptist denomination...* [this gives our children] *an opportunity of receiving an education...*
>
> *(2) Resolved, that the ministers and Deacons of the Concord Baptist Association, in their associate capacity, endorse heartily the plans of Rev. R. McGonagal, D.D., as set forth by him; and will give his enterprise all the support and assistance in our power.*
>
> *(3) Resolved that in view of these things it is expedient to organize a Baptist Church at Boydton, for which purpose the chapel of the College is offered.*

A further resolution was offered to thank the people of the Concord community for "their kindness and hospitality in entertaining those present." This would certainly have included Reverend Leach, who lived less than a mile away from the Concord Church.

But then, a story appears in the February 1872 paper stating that "Dr. McGonegal, President of Southside University, is seriously ill and deranged. Even if his body heals (doubtful) his mind will not." He and his wife, Margaretta, left Boydton and returned to the North. Their first stop was at the home of the Nichols family in Union County, Plainfield, New Jersey. They stayed there for about a month and sold part of the Boydton property to the Nicholses, which was secured by a note from Nichols and Adelberts on August 31, 1872. The McGonegals sold another portion of their holdings to Alex Sydnor of Boydton on September 2, 1872, which closed out their holdings in Mecklenburg County. Henry and Margarette went on to New York City, where Henry died around 1875.

The school in Boydton attempted to reopen in October 1872, led by a Professor Ham, but it was short lived, and no advertisements or news articles were in the paper after February 1872. It appears that Ham moved around 1873 to Clarksville, where he taught in the boys' academy for a couple of years. The property in Boydton went into default and was sold at auction in 1872 but was held in a trust by Colonel Thomas F. Goode, commonwealth's attorney for Mecklenburg County, Virginia.

For the Daniel Leach family, early on in my research, I had found online references in a book, *Lawrence Leach of Salem, Mississippi & Some of His Descendants* by F.B. Phelps Leach, of St. Albans, Vermont, published 1924. But when I coupled this information with that in D. Somners Brown's *Chase City and Its Environs* (1975) and some scattered notes, including from *The American General Biographical Index*, vol. 101, the story was about as clear as mud. Thanks to Fred Leach, who provided me with a copy of some of the pages from *Memoirs of Daniel F. Leach*, I was able to connect all my dots into a story of missionary life in Southside Virginia following the war. There is a significant (to this story) elder brother, Henry L. Leach, who was born on March 6, 1804, and married on November 29, 1829, both in New Milford, Pennsylvania. He and his wife had a son, John Aluano Leach, who was born on March 17, 1853, in New Milford—but more on John later. Another elder brother was Reverend George W. Leach, also a Baptist preacher in New York, who decided against coming to Virginia with Daniel after the war. Of the eleven siblings, Daniel was the only one who came south in 1868.

Daniel Leach married Levantia Guy on May 11, 1841, in Otsego County, Middlefield, New York. She was born there in 1821. The 1850 census record lists the couple living with her parents. Daniel was working as a Baptist preacher, and they had the following children: Henry C., born 1843; Agnes Marilla, born on December 29, 1844; and George Edgar, born on February 28, 1847. All three children were born in Tustin, New York. Thanks to the help of his son, Reverend Henry Curtis Leach, of Hanook Baptist Church in Port Dickenson, New York, a monograph was prepared in 1904 for the fiftieth anniversary of Deposit Baptist Association, New York, entitled *Memoirs of Daniel F. Leach.*

In these records, there is a detailed description of his life in New York. His mother died when he was eleven, and his father followed two years later. Daniel elected as his guardian his uncle Cooper Corbett, who hired him out to a farmer, a Mr. Manley. A short time later, he went to Clarksville, Otsego County, New York, where he apprenticed as a tanner and currier. At the age of fifteen, Daniel believed he was called to the ministry, and he was reluctantly released from his apprenticeship. He alternated between attending school, teaching and working in a printing office in Cooperstown, New York; while there, "hot off the press," the game of baseball was founded by Abner Doubleday (who became a general in the Union army during the Civil War) in 1839. Daniel completed some studies at the Hamilton Literary and Theological Institution (today Colgate).

Daniel preached all over south central New York, often at two churches per day, miles apart, and he would walk the distance (sometimes as much as nineteen miles). From the later 1830s until the early 1850s, he preached all over the Otsego County area and would have been in the throes of the creation of the first baseball club—the New York Knickerbockers—in 1845 by Alexander Cartwright, who also created the fundamental rules of the game. When he relocated about one hundred miles south of Cooperstown in 1854, the Delaware River split his territory. At times this caused him much grief, especially during the rainy season.

He preached for five years at Ten Mile River (present-day Tustin) and five years at Port Jarvis. The remainder of his assignments were one or two years, but he expressed a continuous desire to become a missionary. A sickly man, there would be months that he was unable to get around or travel and he would be on extended sick leaves. Having established several churches, preached thousands of sermons and baptized hundreds of converts, in 1857 he was appointed to the State Baptist Conference as a district missionary. Most of his time was spent in Newark Valley, but he traveled extensively to Yorkshire and New York City, as well as most places in between.

In the winter of 1861–62, he became a missionary of the Broome and Tioga Association. In 1861, he registered for conscription in New York, as a Class 2 (over age forty), in the Nineteenth Congressional District, but it does not appear that he served on active duty in any capacity, not even as chaplain, during the Civil War. In 1862, he returned to Harpersville, New York, where he owned a small farm, and he took over as pastor of the church there but continued to serve as district secretary of the Missionary Board until February 1866. At that time, he was elected as general superintendent of missions for the Baptist Convention of the State of New York. At first, he was appointed "Exploring Missionary," and from his travels throughout New York, he began to write and publish essays on his observations and findings. Many of these were seen as distasteful to the church and not in the best interest of spreading the "message of the Baptists." He was reassigned as a fundraiser for the Society and Missions Board. In January 1868, he returned to preaching for over a year, but much of this time was spent suffering from a debilitating rheumatism. Finally, the family strapped Daniel into an "invalid's chair" and headed south for a better climate. They arrived in Virginia in late spring of 1869.

REVEREND DANIEL LEACH AND
REVEREND CEPHUS DAVIS

L each family historians seem to be somewhat at odds. According to six of the historians on "Family Tree Maker: Ancestor.com" by the Warren and Bonney families of Madison County, New York, Daniel Fowler Leach was born the son of Luther Daniel Leach (October 14, 1777, Torrington, Connecticut) and Eva Corbett (July 15, 1783, Milford, Worchester, Massachusetts). They were married in March 1802 in Corbettsville, Brome County, New York. Eva died on March 27, 1829, in Susquehanna County, New Milford, Pennsylvania, and two years later, Luther died on May 8, 1831, in Corbettesville, New York. They had eleven children, and all are listed as being born in New Milford, Pennsylvania, by six of the historians; but for Daniel, two other family members document Corbettsville, New York, as his birthplace, as do the census records and cemetery headstone. Obviously, Daniel and his wife were traveling about the New York area during his preaching assignments because their fifth, sixth and seventh children were born in a different community—Port Jarvis. They were Alutus, born March 15, 1856; Arkley D., born December 14, 1858; and Marilla, born 1857 but who died soon after arriving in Virginia. Before these was Guydetto, born October 5, 1853, in Harpersville, New York. Guydetto returned to New York, married Jennie Walker and had two children: Lottie and Henry. In 1899, he was working as a mechanic at Eaton, New York.

By 1860, the family was living (according to the census records) in Newark Valley, Tioga, New York, and Daniel was still listed as a Baptist preacher. Arriving in Christiansville, Virginia, in 1869, they must have been steered to the nearest Baptist church: Concord. There, they must have been introduced to Captain Orlando James Hayes, justice of the peace (who became mayor of Chase City in 1886), because on August 23, 1869, Captain Hayes and seven other family members sold a 421-acre parcel of land that bordered the properties of Craddock, Boswell and others to Daniel Leach. The land was located a short walking distance from the church. In those days, there was nothing more than a horse path to the farm, but with development through the years, it is located today at the end of Boondock Road, off Traffic Road in north central Mecklenburg County. It was just across Concord Road but closer to the newly created (1865) Concord Black Church, which is where Leach would be working.

The farm was purchased on Leach's signature, but in February 1870, the purchase price of $2,500 cash was paid in full. In June 1870, the census lists Giles M. Babcock (Leach's son-in-law and business partner) with his wife, Agnes Leach Babcock, and their three-year-old and infant as living next door to Daniel and family. This could be where the money came from to pay off the note. The Babcocks moved on to North Carolina but seemed not to be smitten with the South. Agnes died in Deposit, New York, on July 6, 1875. Her three children in 1899 were Mrs. E. Beulah Babcock Van Noy of Port Jarvis, New York; Elizabeth (Leslie) Leach, a printer and publisher in Chase City; and Fred W. Leach, a farmer in Chase City.

Of the first four children born to Daniel and his wife, they all married people from New York, and Alutus married Mary Luella Hardgrave (August 20, 1862–November 3, 1936), from Canal Fulton, Ohio, who died in Richmond, Virginia. They had four children, the eldest of whom, Edgar Alutus Leach (b. 1888), married Arline Wilson, daughter of William R. Wilson from New York, after the Wilsons moved to Chase City.

Alutus and George Leach were the only two family members of Daniel to call Virginia home for the rest of their lives (Alutus being the only one to remain in Southside). Arkley D. appears to be the only one with a spouse from Virginia, but that's questionable because as soon as he completed dental school, he moved to Knoxville, Tennessee, where he became secretary of a building and loan association. He died on July 12, 1898, in Battle Creek, Michigan. His wife was Mary Walker, and they had three children: Walker, Anua and Robert.

The family in New York was concerned about Daniel. Around 1871, a young new Baptist minister arrived on the scene from New York, full of "fire and brimstone." He was John A. Leach, nephew of Daniel. He was in Chase City to take over the pastorate of the Bethlehem Baptist Church from former pastor Cephus Davis. Bethlehem was a biracial church, which seemed to have been overlooked by the Union army, which occupied Mecklenburg County during its reign of martial law; otherwise, the white citizens would have been made to vacate the premises, such as what happened in Concord. Davis had left the pastorate of the church in an attempt to secure a teaching position with Thyne Institute. The church was in the process of relocating to South Main Street in Chase City (completed in 1874), where a cemetery was developed for its membership. John appears to have remained in Chase City for three or four years and most likely resided with Daniel's family.

Even Reverend John J. Ashenhurst was concerned about the scoundrel Davis being an instructor at the newly forming freedman's Presbyterian school in Chase City. Davis's reputation among the community as a preacher was well known, and this prompted an inquiry from the local Presbyterian Freeman's Board representative, John J. Ashenhurst. The Pittsburg Presbyterian Board contacted the Baptist Home Mission Board of New York, and it in turn elicited Daniel Leach's assistance in investigating Davis, especially his moral turpitude. Daniel found Davis to be a loathsome and self-serving individual. It was discovered that wherever Cephus Davis was preaching or teaching, numerous girls and women became pregnant with his babies (at least thirty were documented by Leach). After two years, Daniel Leach completed his investigation, and in the meantime, Davis had been held in reserve as a teacher.

Daniel sent his report, and as a result, Davis was barred from preaching and teaching. So instead, he ran for a political office on the Democratic ticket and was elected to the House of Delegates in Virginia. "Not a good preacher but an excellent politician" was the sentiment among the black community in Chase City, who elected him into office, according to Douglas Sommers Brown in her book on Chase City. With no money, Cephus Davis reached out to Confederate general William Mahone, formerly of Clarksville, for help in 1878. Mahone furnished Davis with a train ticket to Richmond and, upon his arrival, sent a coach and driver to meet him and deliver him to a fine hotel in Richmond near the capitol. It was reported that he had an elegant room. Soon, he was appointed to the Banking Committee and Privileges and Elections Committees. Within two weeks, he returned to Chase City for a visit. It is said that he was "dressed like a prince with clothes of fine material and the latest fashion, kid gloves and a plug hat." He served one term and was not reelected. He moved to North Carolina, where he tried preaching again but was rejected for a license. He gave a speech at the University of Virginia in 1897 and disappeared after that.

On the surface, it appears that Daniel's failing health didn't improve with the Southside climate. He was described as a tireless worker, slender in statue, and it was said he "never enjoyed robust health." His only documented work locally was that he attended the Concord black church, and off and on, he did teach Sunday school there. But the "fire and brimstone" of New York was not seen in Mecklenburg County. No preaching, no new churches and no souls converted. Is this an enigma, or is there a logical explanation? In New York, he was a supporter of temperance, and he was "an anti-slavery agitator. He had large evangelistic gifts, and more than ordinary pulpit ability." He wrote numerous religious papers and a book that was published by the American Baptist Publishing Society in 1887, and he was working on a book on Mormonism. He may have been a preacher, teacher and writer, but all this took place in New York. It is really obvious that after a very short period of time, Daniel must have realized that coming to Southside Virginia as a missionary was a mistake.

He returned to New York in the summer of 1871 to "recharge his batteries" and began preaching at two churches again. "He was quite crippled by rheumatism," was "unable to use one hand, and we assisted him at the table." He returned to Virginia before Christmas, and it would seem that he brought with him a revived energy, as well as his nephew John A. Leach. He went to the Mecklenburg County courthouse and, as recorded in Deed Book 39, took an oath and registered with the county as a "Minister of the Baptist Faith" on July 15, 1872, for the purpose of performing marriage ceremonies.

Upon his return, "here his interest and sympathy were greatly stirred by the condition of the colored citizens. They had been thrust out of the white churches…and left without organization or instruction as to church order, choice of pastors, elections, deacons, or trustees, holding of property, etc. He was…laboring among the colored people in Mecklenburg, Lunenburg or Charlotte counties. The records of the society show that during this time he preached 1,193 sermons, baptized 1,089 persons and organized five churches." He also trained black preachers, ordained pastors and guided them in association work from 1872 to about 1880.

But following the inquest of Cephus Davis, publication of the findings and the banishment of Davis from the ministry—guilty or not guilty—it was time to run the Leaches out of town. After all, they had "attacked and demeaned" one of the most prominent preachers in the county. By 1878, John was back preaching in New York. Daniel was invited to appear at the annual Concord Baptist Association meeting in August 1878. At this meeting, a resolution was passed that the association, "being in full sympathy with our brother, D.F. Leach, Missionary of the A.B[aptist] H[ome] Mission

Society (among the colored people in our section of the state), and we bid him Godspeed." Not a bad "Get out of town" note...was it an attempted rescue?

Daniel stayed as long as he could, but finally, sometime before 1883, he left his family in Virginia and returned home to New York. He toured several of his old churches and again became the pastor of the Newark Valley church in December 1883. He remained there until April 1888. He retired, returned to Virginia and died at home suddenly on September 10, 1889. (Again, the historians disagree. Seven say he died in Concord, Virginia. They don't know it was the Concord community, not the town). A parcel or parcels of the farm were sold because the final estate in 1889 was 375 acres. Following Daniel's death, Levantia did not remarry. She lived out her last days with Alutus and his family until her death in 1899. There is a notation in the *Chase City Progress* that in 1898, she visited her family in Wytheville, Virginia, and in 1898, they came to Chase City to visit her.

WHAT'S THE REAL STORY BEHIND THE NAMING OF THE TOWN OF CHASE CITY?

Word traveled fast, and by 1874, many stories in Pennsylvania, New York and Ohio were referring to Chase City as the "richest northern town in the south." The town was evolving rapidly, with new families arriving monthly from the North. Cheap land, fertile soil, southern climate and room to breathe and create one's own destiny were just some of the advertised inducements touted by the board of settlers who had organized to advertise and bring in new citizens. The first two primary settlers who came to the community for the purpose of developing and building this dream, following the Civil War, were George Endly and his brother-in-law John G. Boyd. Endly purchased the 1,350-acre parcel of Richard C. Puryear, complete with home, store and other property, referred to as "The City." Adjacent parcels totaling over 3,000 acres were purchased by him and John G. Boyd before 1871. The original 1,350-acre parcel was surveyed, platted and parceled with a town plan detailed in the drawings. But what to name the town?

Coincidentally, their longtime friend and mentor Salmon P. Chase, who was serving on the Supreme Court and had been assigned the role of presiding justice over the impeachment trial of President Andrew Johnson, suffered from a heart attack or stroke and was staying with a friend in Richmond. Boyd and Endly decided it would be the right time to visit their ailing friend and to possibly spread his legacy into the South. The following have been retyped from the news stories that appeared in the May 8 and 15, 1873 issues of the *Mecklenburg Herald*, written by Langston Easley Finch, E.A. Baptist and J.A.H. St. Andrew, Esq. There were a total of five stories and the first, titled *"New York Times* Correspondent of Richmond Remarks on Naming of Chase City," was published May 15, 1873. It stated:

Salmon P. Chase is in Richmond for respite with the "rebel," General Bradley Johnson. He has not made his appearance in public, and many wonder the occasion of his visit. A number of Englishmen, who reside in Mecklenburg County, recently named a village they have settled "Chase City" after the Chief Justice…Chase City Colony was started by Northerners. Englishmen and Scotchmen have since come in and are helping to build up the city, but the proportion of Northerners to English in the district is as fifteen to one.

Another editorial was titled "The Death of the Chief Justice":

By the death of Mr. Chase the nation has been deprived of a statesman, wise and [unreadable]. *Stainless and pure; a Chief Judge whose ermine was spotless; a citizen whose record was the history of lofty aims and high purposes accomplished. It is an awful fact—a fact which should convey a terrible meaning to us all—that there are within the range of American politics but few men whose characters can be classed with that of the Chief Justice. It is the stern duty of every citizen to decide that only politicians as just and honest as Mr. Chase shall be placed in the chief offices of the nation. It may be that the Chief Justice was almost the last of the true patriots holding national distinctions. Politics reduced to the level of a huckster's stall; demand immediate and total reformation and while the nation mourns for a noble citizen the people are called on to decree.*

To Mecklenburg County, which by the incorporation of Chase City, had recently established a friendly association with the Chief Justice, the loss of Mr. Chase is of no ordinary importance. In him we had a friend whose ability to help us was as powerful as his desire to assist us was undoubted. Within a few days of his death he rendered an essential service to Chase City at Washington, and among his latest letters was the following, addresses to the Southside Virginia Board of Settlers:

"Washington, May 1ˢᵗ, 1873
"Gentlemen—I have delayed too long my reply to your Address, received some weeks since, and must now be brief.

The complete restoration of the Southern States to their former prosperity and their advancement in their new life to a prosperity heretofore unknown, must be the ardent wish of every patriotic citizen.

The success of such enterprises as that in which the Southside Virginia Board of Settlers are engaged will ensure the result to which all good men look forward with hope. I am gratified by the spark of personal esteem of which you inform me and consent with pleasure to such use of my name in connection with the Board as you propose.

Very truly yours, S.P. Chase"

So long as the great work of resettling Virginia needs to be prosecuted the noble words of Chief Justice Chase will furnish the Board of Settlers with a glorious motto and a grand incentive to increase diligence in their patriotic labors.

Endly, having purchased the estate of Richard C. Puryear, was well aware that the crossroads of Boydton Courthouse Road and Abbeyville Road had been mapped as "The City" since the 1830s. As hard as Puryear appears to have tried, the Christiansville Post Office remained, even after he purchased and moved the businesses and his family home. For example, on May 21, 1861, the circuit court ordered the hands of John M. Hayes to do the road work, of which James H. Dodson was surveyor, leading from Scott's old shop at the crossroads and intersecting with the road from the city to the edge of Thomas W. Hayes's property, between Wm. R. Burton and lands of W. Hayes.

In his inventory of personal possessions to settle the estate following his death in 1863, it is noted that the Christiansville Postal Desk was in his home. Chase's letter provided the authorization for the board of settlers to add "Chase" to "The City" after receiving his letter. Chase never knew that Chase City had been named and incorporated before April 1, 1873.

By 1909, Chase City could boast of six hotels and at least four substantial boardinghouses. In the 1940s, there were six automobile dealerships. With a railroad station, two major bus line stations and the new age of automobile travel, Chase City had become the shopping mecca of the Piedmont region.

GONE WITH THE WIND BEGAN
IN THE PIEDMONT

Myrta Lockett was born in Mecklenburg County, Virginia, in 1857 to Harwood Alexander Lockett (b. 1812 to circa 1900). Harwood was from Halifax County and was the nephew of Revolutionary War soldier Royal Lockett, who had settled in Mecklenburg County before 1800. Harwood was a respected businessman at a young age and had served on many occasions as surety for claims by persons against Buffalo Springs Resort as early as 1830. In September 1832, Harwood was appointed a deputy sheriff for Mecklenburg County. He began work at the Buffalo Mineral Springs Resort around 1830, but in 1833, he moved to Clarksville, where he continued to be a deputy but was also managing an ordinary. He was still in Clarksville in 1840. His brother Stephan owned the steam-powered sawmill on First Street and was the Clarksville town constable. His first cousin Henry, who had graduated from Randolph Macon College in 1838, had purchased a farm next door to the college farm and was farming and serving as a financial agent for the college. In 1847, Henry was elected major of the Twenty-second Regiment, Fifteenth Battalion, of the Mecklenburg County militia.

Around 1850, Harwood took over management of the Lombardy Grove Ordinary. Because of an increase in travel due to a new stagecoach line in 1850, the Boydton to Petersburg Plank Toll Road in the early 1850s and the growth of both R.M. College and Buffalo Springs Resort, Jacob Holt was hired in 1858 by the owner, William Baskervill, to repair, remodel and add twenty additional guest rooms to the ordinary. The total cost from Holt was $1,640; with this, the ordinary became a hotel. Harwood must have returned to Halifax County during the construction, and that would explain why some local historians suggest that Myrta was born there rather than at Lombardy Grove. Her brother, Phillip Lockett, was born in Mecklenburg County, in 1842.

Phillip, a nineteen-year-old student from R.M. College, enlisted into Company F, Fourteenth Virginia Infantry, as a private at Lombardy Grove on May 12, 1861. He was a junior in mathematics but also received a diploma in French in 1861. He was one of the four students involved in writing a scathing letter of protest on April 3, 1861, to the R.M. College Board of Trustees. He was expelled because of this but appealed his case and received demerits instead.

Harwood Lockett also had a ward who was attending the Danville Female College in 1865 when President Davis came to town. His daughter Myrta wrote:

> *Knowing that Danville might become a fighting center, Mr. Williams T. Davis, (President of the Danville Female College) wrote my father (Harwood) to send for Sue (the trusted and esteemed family servant). The way to reach Danville was by private conveyance, seventy miles or more. Uncle Dick (the family coachman), mounted high on the carriage-box, a white-headed, black-faced knight-errant of chivalry, set forth…In due time the carriage rolled into the yard (of the girls school), Uncle Dick proud and happy on his box, Sue inside wrapped in rugs, sound asleep, for it was midnight.*

Phillip was captured and made a prisoner of war at Gettysburg on July 3, 1863. He was sent to Fort Delaware and then transferred to Fort McHenry on July 7, 1863. On August 1, 1863, he was transferred to City Point and exchanged. Returning to his company, he was elected first lieutenant on April 6, 1864. At the Battle of Bermuda Hundred, he received gunshot wounds to the neck and shoulder on June 19, 1864. He was admitted to Richmond General Hospital on June 19, 1864, and sent home to Lombardy Grove for a furlough on August 10, 1864. Returning to his company, he signed the company clothing invoices on November 30, 1864, as the company commander. He was paroled at Appomattox on April 9, 1865. He returned home to pursue his education, with an *Artium Magister* degree, R.M. College. In 1869, he began a successful law practice, with offices in Lombardy Grove and Boydton. He was elected and served as commonwealth's attorney for Mecklenburg County from July 1, 1875, to 1879.

Myrta spent many hours on her father's knee in the family tavern, also known as "Delony's Ordinary" (the name of the original owner), in Lombardy Grove during the war. She was mesmerized listening to the war stories of her father, her brothers and travelers. In 1867, Lombardy Grove was sold and the Lockett family moved to Petersburg. Following her schooling, she spent a number of years traveling while serving as a relief worker in China and Cuba. Returning to the United States, she settled in Atlanta, Georgia. In 1884, she married Dr. James Corban Avary, a physician in Atlanta. There she was a writer for the *Atlanta Journal*, *Atlanta Constitution* and *Atlanta Georgian*. In the 1890s, they moved to New York.

Her first book project was assisting her father with writing his autobiography, *The Diary of Harwood Alexander Lockett*, which was published in 1895. In 1903, Myrta's first book was published, *A Virginia Girl in the Civil War* (New York, 1903), followed by *Dixie after the War: 1861–1865* (New York, 1906). She also edited and caused to be published the war diary of Mrs. James Chesnut Jr. (Mary Boykin Chesnut) of South Carolina, *Diary from Dixie*. But probably her most successful book was *Diary of Alexander H. Stevens, Vice President of the Confederacy, during His Imprisonment in Ft. Warren*, circa 1910. Following the publication of this book, she filed for a legal separation from Dr. Avary in New York.

She became very active in the Salvation Army in New York and also worked with the Woman's War Relief Association during World War I. Her last published book was *Uncle Remus and the Wren's Nest*, but this was not the end of her writing career. According to Margaret Mitchell, who wrote *Gone with the Wind*, one of her progenitors and inspirations for writing the book was Myrta Lockett Avary. Mrs. Avary died on February 14, 1946, having returned to live out her days in Atlanta.

Much of her correspondence and other documents from 1868 to 1931 are with the Kanan Research Center, Atlanta History Center. This includes several collections of memoirs from 1941 written for her son, John Kennon Lockett, and her sister-in-law Lulie Baskervill Lockett. Papers include correspondence regarding copies at the varying stages of publication of her books, numerous unpublished poems and other unpublished writings. It is important to note that while residing in Mecklenburg County, her neighbor also became a noted writer about the same era of Southern and Civil War history: Edna Turpin.

Less than ten miles to the west of Lombardy Grove was a plantation named Echo Hill, owned by Edward Henry and Petronella Lee Turpin. They had moved to the area from Powhatan, Virginia, to be part of the horse community. On July 26, 1867, Edna Henry Lee Turpin was born. Her father died in 1870, and in 1871, her mother married William C. Johnson, who had the remnants of a plantation (880 acres), and the family moved there. The plantation of Echo Hill was sold in October 1871.

A Presbyterian, Edna attended and graduated from Hollins College in Virginia. She returned home and eventually purchased the Echo Hill Plantation home (but with the railroad passing through the property in 1890, it was then referred to as Antlers, with a railroad station, post office and country store) and several hundred acres of land. She kept the home for many years, although it served primarily as a vacation home. In 1925, she was commissioned by the Mecklenburg County Board of Supervisors to attend the Virginia Historical Commission conference in Richmond, to work with them on documenting the soldiers from Mecklenburg County who served in World War I. She was paid thirty-five dollars to help cover her expenses.

Edna's first short story was published in 1882, when she was fifteen. Her writings appealed to the adolescent market, but she was regarded as a significant history writer. Some of her work includes several school textbooks and *History of the American People, Honey Sweet, Happy Acres, Peggy of Roundabout Lane, Three Circus Days* and many others. She died on June 8, 1952, and was buried in the family plot in Hollywood Cemetery, Richmond, Virginia. The Virginia Historical Society in Richmond has a significant amount of her writings and papers, both published and unpublished. Hollins College (University) held her in high regard, and today, there is a campus park named in her honor.

THE TWENTIETH CENTURY

THE VIRGILINA GOLD VEIN IS REOPENED AND MINING RETURNS TO THE PIEDMONT

A gold mining company from New York and another from Pennsylvania converged on Southside in the 1890s. In 1900, investors built a luxurious hotel/sanitarium with 150 rooms and twenty-five thousand acres of riding trails for recreation, sport and hunting in the town of Chase City. The trains came to Chase City, deposited the mining executives and their families for accommodation and then headed to the mining areas in the Virgilina District, Halifax County, Virginia, and Granville County, North Carolina. When working the mines, trains departed Chase City at 7:00 a.m. and returned from Virgilina, Virginia, at 5:00 p.m. In 1894, Virgilina began a newspaper called the *Silver Dollar*. But the mining executives thought the Virgilina community too raucous for their own families to stay there.

Two individuals spoke and wrote about their professional experiences with the mining operations. One was Frank Clemens Smith, PhD. Dr. Smith was a professor of mining engineering at the University of Michigan when recruited and hired to work in Virgilina. In 1910, he moved to Chase City, purchased an antebellum plantation, Reveille, and would parade down Main Street telling everyone that he was a millionaire from his investment in the mines. He died in 1931.

Another individual was less flamboyant: Jack Robbins. Robbins was from eastern Tennessee. He arrived in Virgilina around 1900. When most of the mines closed about 1912, he stayed, purchased a farm and started mining his own property. He did this for several years with no other source of income but

Mecklenburg Mineral Springs Hotel and Sanitarium, July 4, 1904. This was the first major July 4 celebration in Southside since 1860, featuring a reenactment of the charge at San Juan Hill. *Courtesy of William C. Gregory.*

Reveille Plantation manor house, circa 1840. The two men in front are probably Charles Haskins, owner, and a guest in this 1890s photograph. *Courtesy of Deborah Magann.*

With tunnels at three hundred to five hundred feet underground, track has been laid and an unidentified man is using an ore car to haul the rock to the elevator or to the surface. *Courtesy of Greg B. Reese.*

always stated he was unsuccessful. But then he would clarify what he meant by saying he was "unsuccessful at finding a vein." The mystery of the closing of the mines still remains. What prompted the closing in 1912 for most (over twenty) of the mines? Were they really depleted? Still, five or six continued operation until 1944, and they were the only mines to extend their tunnels from an average of twenty feet to over two hundred feet deep.

On July 27, 1903, the Mecklenburg County Board of Supervisors was given a challenge by Colonel Thomas F. Goode, attorney and owner of the Buffalo Mineral Springs Resort. He pledged $2,500 to the county for the purpose of hiring a competent miner and metallurgist to explore the lands of the county for metals, and he would be glad for the board of supervisors to supplement the same. Finally, on March 12, 1906, the board instructed the superintendent of the poorhouse to secure an ore sample from the poorhouse farm lands to be sent for an assay. There is no further reference of this in the board's records, but at the meeting of the board on January 4, 1910, the poorhouse farm had to refund $37.09 to the board as being overpaid. They did so with gold. At the July 1910 meeting, Thomas J. Williams Sr., the poorhouse superintendent, resigned (although he had previously retired in 1905), effective July 1, 1911.

In 1955, "a Canadian mining company, one of the largest in the world, assessed the area for quite some time." It leased seven thousand acres but has

Preparations are underway for digging a new tunnel. Two unidentified men have placed a ceiling support and have begun to excavate the rock wall. *Courtesy of Greg B. Reese.*

not returned, despite several correspondences between the commonwealth and the company over the years. I am not privy as to why. The company's primary focus was the Virgilina District, which spans from five miles south of Virgilina, Virginia, into Granville County, North Carolina, and north across the eastern edge of Halifax County, then through the center of Charlotte County, Virginia, through Drakes Branch (especially Horsepen Creek, and Little Horsepen area) and on to Keysville, crossing literally hundreds of streams and six rivers throughout the trip.

In Halifax County, Virginia, the Red Bank Mine, owned primarily by the Hamme brothers, was the most profitable gold mine and the longest operating. It was the only gold mine still in operation at the time of the survey (1917) and the only one to be fully developed into its own community in the area. "In 1912 it was reported the mine had produced $22,000 worth of gold, according to Reverend Mathis, and in the 1940s, gold was produced in commercial quantity from the Red Bank Mine, along with a small quantity of copper."

The production yard of the Hamme Tungsten Mine in Vance County, North Carolina, seen here in 1955, includes the office, tower and machining operations, much like the Red Bank Mine in Halifax County, Virginia. *Courtesy of Greg B. Reese.*

According to the U.S. Department of the Interior, Geological Survey Bulletin #948-A, in the 1940s, the federal government had staff conduct an investigation of the mines. It was reported that "their recommendations were favorable to mining." Throughout the survey of the mines, William Laney, the lead surveyor, stated that "the ore is available and the productivity should be profitable." The primary rock formations that Laney could decipher were "granite and schist with numerous quartz veins." With all the federal employees surveying the area, at one point they got sidetracked and began doing more surveying south of the river (present-day lake) where tungsten was discovered in 1901.

Their report contains a description that the vein is eight miles by eight miles and extends from Townsville, North Carolina, to the lake and north of it and then west toward Nelson, Virginia. These mines were dug to a depth of several hundred feet and required a lot more equipment than did the gold, silver, copper and kaolin mines. But alas, these mines were also abandoned sometime after 1955 due to the completion of the flood plan reservoir program by the Corps of Engineers. One of the last mines to close was the Hammes brothers' mine, Hamme Tungsten Mine, in Vance County, North Carolina.

DR. ADAM TYREE FINCH SR. AND THREE HOSPITALS IN SOUTHSIDE

D
r. Adam Tyree Finch Sr. became a legend while alive and working in Chase City. He was born at his parents' home near Chase City on February 29, 1872. Graduating from public schools, he attended Virginia Polytechnic Institute (VPI), graduating with his bachelor's degree in 1893. He transferred to the University of Virginia medical department and completed the program there, becoming a medical doctor in 1896. He was offered and accepted the position of clinical medicine instructor, working in that capacity until 1898. In 1898, he returned to VPI as commandant of cadets and professor of physiology until 1901. He left the university and served as physician in residence at the Buffalo Mineral Springs resort, working for Colonel Thomas F. Goode until 1902, when the mining in the Virgilina District was in full swing. In that year, he returned to Chase City and established both a medical practice and a pharmacy but continued his seasonal practice at Buffalo Springs until October 1903. It should also be stated that the Mecklenburg Mineral Springs Hotel and Sanitarium opened for business in 1902, and Dr. Finch was listed as a stockholder, medical consultant and house physician on call.

In the pharmacy, his business partner was William H. Pettus. Dr. Finch and Pettus hired a Mr. Booker for a short time to get the store operating and functional. Pettus was soon replaced by James Price, pharmacist, who maintained operation of the store for nearly twenty years. Dr. Finch's home on the family plantation on the Black Branch Road burned in 1900 and was not rebuilt. Almost as soon as Dr. Finch reached age twenty-one, he

Mecklenburg Mineral Springs Hotel and Sanitarium was completed in 1902 but burned in 1909. It included twenty-five thousand acres of land for sport. *Courtesy of Southside Regional Library, Boydton.*

was in Chase City selling real estate, consisting of lots and parcels of his grandparents' farm. He was also buying and selling lots from John Boyd and George Endley, the founders/developers of the town.

On July 7, 1899, Dr. Finch and Elizabeth ("Bessie") D. Morton were married in Chase City, and their firstborn child was Mary W. Finch in 1901, and then came Elizabeth M. Finch in 1902 and Margaret G. Finch in 1904. The family built and settled into their new home on Boyd Street about 1905, but it is unclear if they lived in the grandparents' home for several years before moving there. In the census of 1910, the family is living in their new home with two black servant girls named Rosa Roberts (age eighteen) and Nannie (age nineteen). Also living in the home was Finch's mother-in-law, Mrs. S.H. Morton, age sixty-eight and widowed. Two more children were added to the family: Adam T. Finch Jr. in 1906 and William C. Finch in December 1909.

Dr. Finch was a prolific writer, having published professional articles in both the Virginia and the American Medical Societies' journals. He also wrote *Hand Book* for the University of Virginia, which the university published. Returning to Chase City, he became one of the leading forces in organizing the Mecklenburg Guard, which was attached to the 72nd Virginia Regiment, with sixty-four men and three officers. First Captain Adam T. Finch was the commanding officer. It became Company E, 116th Regiment of the Virginia

National Guard in September 1903. This is where his residence comes into question, because the grandparents' home, which he had inherited, still stands (though in very sad shape). When visiting the home, the old driveway for the doctor's buggy is still visible and connects Barnesville Road (present-day Fifth Street) and the Black Branch Road. Finch would have quick access to the north and south of town. It is pretty obvious that this roadway was well used, though barely visible today.

Being the commanding officer and having served as commandant of a military-style unit at VPI, Finch knew his men needed a place to train, first and foremost. The only old postcard photos that I have seen are from around 1911 and show Company E training in the front yard of his grandparents' farmhouse. Also, if one walks into the woods, directly across the pasture in front of the house, he or she will come to a branch that feeds Little Bluestone Creek. On the south side of that branch is a dirt mound that partially covers a cement wall, which served as the target area of a shooting range for the company. (Of course, the argument could be made that his home on Boyd Street, which he built in 1904, was only about five blocks to the east of the range, but then that house became a hospital in 1921.) In any event, the company also needed an indoor area to carry on business, and in 1909, Dr. Finch was instrumental in securing monies from donations, the town and county sufficient to build a Chase City Armory on Main Street. (Just a reminder, in 1909 and 1911, there were no paved streets in town, no electricity and no sewer system.)

Dr. Finch was a devout Methodist from a longstanding family of the same. He was heavily involved with carrying out the work of the YMCA, both in spiritual meetings and in aid programs. He was one of those responsible for helping to organize, build and establish the First Christian Church in Chase City in 1929. One of his daughters, Mary, became a missionary with the Methodist Episcopal South Conference. One of his sons, William C. Finch, went on to become renowned in his own right as a grand and useful president of several Methodist colleges throughout the South during some of their most troubled times.

The fair had begun in 1904 with the Mecklenburg Mineral Springs Hotel hosting a fall Agricultural Exhibit possibly inspired by Dr. Finch. After the hotel burned in 1909 and after nearly a year of cleanup, the Agricultural Exhibit expanded to a fair in 1910 on the newly graded site of the old hotel. But it wasn't until August 1911 that the Mecklenburg County Agricultural Fair Association became incorporated and purchased its own property. In 1911, Dr. Finch moved into another passionate pursuit, that being the South

Central Virginia Agricultural Fair, and he was appointed the Chase City member of the board of directors and was elected by the board as a first vice-president.

But there was gloom in the near future. In 1916, Company E of the Mecklenburg Guard was activated and sent to fight along the Mexican border in Brownsville, Texas. After seven months, the soldiers returned to Chase City only to be activated again in 1917, but this time they would be going to Europe to participate in World War I. They were first sent to New Jersey for readiness training, and then they were sent to France, where they served for over eighteen months. Dr. Finch was reestablished from commanding officer of the company of the Mecklenburg Guard as a captain and promoted to staff surgeon with the rank of major in Company E, 116th Infantry, U.S. Army. Following the war, Company E returned to Newport News, Virginia, where the men were discharged on May 28 and 29, 1919. Included among them was the only Medal of Honor recipient from Virginia during World War I, Lucius Gregory, although he was transferred to a different unit when they arrived in Europe. While in France, Dr. Finch's orderly from Chase City, William L. Rockwell, was killed in action.

During the war, Mrs. A.T. Finch headed up a program at the armory in Chase City in which local wives and others prepared bandages and knitted goods to send to the troops overseas. Returning to the United States, Dr. Finch was offered a position with the new Walter Reed Army Hospital in Washington, D.C., but he chose to come home. Upon his return, he was appointed as one of the county health officers, and he almost immediately began making preparations for a hospital in town. The results were that he added a wing and a few other modifications to the family home and converted that to the Chase City Hospital, which opened in June 1921. He had two physicians who came to town on prescribed days, and his backup physician was Dr. Clarence Saunders of Chase City. From this hospital, which also conducted nurses' training, numerous babies were delivered, bones set and lives saved.

On many occasions, Dr. Finch appeared before town council requesting, among other things, the "Opera House" for use to host or plan events for both the YMCA and the National Guard. He was so commonplace at meetings that he was elected to town council from 1923 to 1925, during which time he was instrumental in securing an American Legion hall in Chase City. At that time, he was also on the water and sewer committee to bring these needed services to the town so that they would be safe for the citizens. After all, in 1917, the State Department of Health condemned both the town wells and

Chase City Hospital is pictured in 1921 on Boyd Street. The medical director and owner was Dr. Adam Finch, and the hospital closed in 1930. *Courtesy of William C. Gregory.*

the sewer system, but the town council refused to appropriate the necessary funds for needed corrections.

Of the seven nurses who were trained at the Chase City Hospital, two were Finch's daughters, Margaret and Elizabeth Goode Finch. The hospital closed on March 1, 1930, and soon thereafter, Drs. Finch and Saunders died, as did Dr. Saunders's wife, Adelia, who was the first female pharmacist in the commonwealth of Virginia. She was owner of Chase City Drug Store from 1888 until 1930. In 1946, his son Dr. Adam Finch Jr. built a new hospital on Marshall Street. Dr. Finch Sr. had served a total of seventeen years with the National Guard and was a lieutenant colonel when he died. The hospital became an apartment building following the Depression and, in 1969 and 1970, served as the temporary Chase City Private School. Subsequently, the building was razed.

SOUTH CENTRAL FAIR ASSOCIATION, INC.

In 2010, the South Central Fair celebrated one hundred years of operation and entertainment. The original organizers were T.E. Roberts, president; Dr. A.T. Finch, first vice-president; J.A. Robertson, treasurer; and C.E. Geoghegan, secretary and general manager. The fair had an office on Fourth Street. Other Southside regional vice-presidents were B.D. Adams, Red Oak; John T. Lewis, Clarksville; W.M. Winn, Skipwith; C.S. Gordan, Union Level; H.L. Petty, North View; R.B. Brenneman, Drakes Branch; P.H. Dodson, Ontario; and D.B. Goode, Chase City. Directors included T.E. Roberts, A.T. Finch, W.H. Jeffreys Jr., J.A. Robertson, Lucius Gregory, N.H. Williams, R.D Patterson and C.E. Geoghegan.

Mecklenburg County had actually begun a fair in 1871. The president and founder of the fair was Colonel William Townes Sr. Following the Civil War, Southside Virginia was under the close scrutiny of military martial law by the United States Army. In late 1870, the counties in Virginia were required to create and elect a county board of supervisors to govern the county, as prescribed by the federal government. Finally, following the results and implementation of that election, the U.S. troops left. To celebrate the newly acquired freedom of the county, Colonel Townes formed a group that began a Mecklenburg County farmers' fair in celebration. It was held on the property of the vacant Randolph Macon College, near Cox Road. The first fair was held in September 1872, with farmers bringing in produce for "bragging rights" and their wives cooking and baking for the same reason. The fair grew in popularity until 1875, when Colonel Townes became ill. It was discontinued after that year, and in 1876, Colonel Townes died.

The fair had begun again in 1904, with the Mecklenburg Mineral Springs Hotel hosting a fall Agricultural Exhibit in an effort to stimulate business. But due to a lack of facilities and stables for the animals, T.E. Roberts purchased a 20.4-acre parcel on behalf of the fair association. This became known as the "Fair Farm" and was located on the Barnesville Road (present-day Fifth Street). Then, in August 1911, the Mecklenburg County Agricultural Fair Association became incorporated and purchased property. The new fairgrounds were dedicated in the fall of 1912.

To promote the fair and expand its appeal, a more regional approach was adopted in both the advertising and the operations personnel (including the directors and vice-presidents). The fair association also approached the county board of supervisors for several counties to solicit their support and endorsements. The association approached the Mecklenburg County Board of Supervisors and requested funds to build exhibits and stockhouses. The association estimated a need of $350. The decision of the board members was evenly split, with four both for and against. They approached circuit court judge C.J. Faulkner to break the tie, and he voted yes, but with a proviso: the county would receive a deed to the one and one-half acres of land and buildings (that is why the buildings were built on the border, instead of the middle, of the property). That way, if the fair did not succeed, the county could sell its assets. The fair association was granted first option to purchase the buildings and property from the county, which it did in 1946. The association received the $350 in July 1912. Having completed livestock houses in 1914, the "Fair Farm" was sold to James Farrar in November 1914, and he built a home there.

I am not aware of the actions of other counties, other than the recommended vice-presidents and directors being appointed, but Mecklenburg County was supportive. The board of supervisors appropriated money each year (ranging from $100 to begin and then $150 annually, following the Depression) from April 1913 and into the late 1940s (when I stopped reading board of supervisors records).

The first brochure advertising the fair reads:

Chase City is an ideal place to hold the County Fair, it being the most central point of the counties of Mecklenburg, Lunenburg and Charlotte, is accessible from all directions. Its people are hospitable, enterprising and wide-a-wake to the interests of all people of the state.

We cordially tender an invitation to everyone to attend this Fair and feel sure that whether you come as an exhibitor or spectator, you will return to your homes well pleased, instructed and rewarded. So come, bring your neighbors and let's have a good old time together.

The South Central Fair draws a crowd from all over the Piedmont. This was a fairway display of the new line of 1950 Ford automobiles. *Courtesy of Carolyn Duke Shearin.*

The annual contributions by the Mecklenburg County Board of Supervisors made to the fair association allowed it to provide prize money to be awarded to individuals, especially schoolchildren, who would be judged in numerous categories. Some categories were awarded prize ribbons, and some would also win a cash award. But whatever the prize, it was received with excitement and bragging rights by the participant. Horses are still a big part of the community and the fair parade.

I can personally remember entering an insect collection into the fair when I was in the eighth grade in 1961. I won a blue ribbon for first place and a check for one dollar. I was so proud of that accomplishment, and I still have the ribbon in my personal scrapbook.

The late Dwight L. Moody Jr. (minister, song writer and champion fiddle player) wrote his autobiography in 2001. Born on December 26, 1929, he was still performing, recording music and managing his recording company in Charlotte, North Carolina, until his death in 2013. A radio and TV personality, he has three times been nominated for a Grammy award. One of his fond memories of Mecklenburg County (he is from LaCrosse) that he writes about in his book is of the county fair. He says, "The Mecklenburg County Fair always had school entries. In

Left: The fair parade was a welcome event and a pep rally for the fair. Horses are still part of Southside. This is Finch Parker riding Black Magic on Main Street at the former Chase City Post Office in 1962. *Courtesy of Tommy Parker.*

Below: Times have changed from new car exhibits, horses and jumping to old cars, horsepower and the feature attraction of demolition derby. *Courtesy of Dora Garner, South Central Fair Association, Inc.*

1938, I won 1st place in writing, with a Blue Ribbon, and 25 cents. Boy, was I proud."

The South Central Fair Association, Inc., is still going strong at this writing in 2013, although the entertainment venue has changed over the years, as have the attractions and rides. It continues to serve the Piedmont region after over one hundred years.

KIBLERVILLE

John Adam Kibler (September 5, 1851–October 4, 1942) was the youngest son of David Kibler (1804–1881) and Hann Shaffer Kibler (1804–1894). They were from Page County (formerly part of Shenandoah County), Virginia, and were part of a prominent pioneer family that settled the Shenandoah Valley in the 1770s. The Kibler family members served in the military during the Revolutionary War and Civil War, and many were merchants, physicians and ministers, but all were farmers. I have found three books that have been written about the Kibler family, and numerous other books about the Shenandoah Valley also included chapters referencing the family.

As a young woman, Ann Virginia "Jennie" Mathers, from Mecklenburg County, was apparently vacationing near the Luray Caverns, which were under development in 1879. It seems that there, she met John Kibler, and on March 20, 1880, they were married. From this marriage were six children born in Warren County, Virginia: William Daniel "Magnus" Kibler, born on December 20, 1880; Joseph Abraham Kibler, born on July 12, 1882; Hattie Ann Kibler, born on July 21, 1884; Manton Mahone Kibler, born on October 4, 1887, and died on February 9, 1967, in Henrico County; Bertha Mabel Kibler, born on October 10, 1890; and John Lee Kibler, born on January 17, 1893.

Following the death of John's mother in 1894, the family moved to Mecklenburg County to be closer to Jennie's family. They purchased a farm on Wightman Road, next to the Meherrin River, and established a successful business operation. John Adam was a wagoner by trade, and he both built and repaired wagons. He was also a blacksmith. He built a grinding mill for grains, and with the help of Magnus, they operated a stave mill for cooperage in 1898. He taught his sons these skills, and Jennie taught them school subjects.

Edna Cloe Kibler was born to John and Jennie in Mecklenburg County in 1897. This was followed by the birth of their youngest child, James M. Kibler, on April 18, 1900. By 1910, Magnus was running the businesses, John L. was overseeing the farm, Bertha was taking care of the home and Edna and James were home (not in school). Joseph was not in the home. It seems that he was with his first cousin, Joseph Milton Kibler (b. April 21, 1883, in Shenandoah County), and they were working in the fertilizer/mercantile business of Walter Simmons in Union Level, Mecklenburg County, Virginia.

On September 9, 1913, the postmaster general of the United States Post Office Department, A.S. Burleson, appointed Joseph A. Kibler to the position of postmaster for the Mecklenburg County Post Office at Reddirt. Kibler was to replace the retiring postmaster, Jesse A. Barden. The appointment was a paid position with the federal government, with a salary of $200 per month (quite a sum for the day), and it included an allowance of $200 to construct a new post office building (as Barden owned the former). An audit was conducted of Barden's books, and Joseph Kibler, a single man, opened the new post office on September 30, 1913. It was a frame building, twenty by forty feet, located on five acres that Kibler had purchased at the intersection of Coleman Road and Reddirt (though neither road nor community exist today, other than to the local hunt club). The post office served as a country store and the backroom as living quarters. Outside the store, Joseph had a blacksmith setup, and on the creek, below the store, he had built a small grinding mill.

Also in 1913, Manton Mahone Kibler, age twenty-five, purchased a parcel of land on Concord Road and established a wagon repair/blacksmith business. Over the next seven years, he purchased five more parcels of land, primarily from the Coleman and Garner families. Joseph Kibler operated the store/post office until the U.S. Postal Department closed it on April 30, 1916. In 1917, Kibler returned to Page County and married Mary Elizabeth Compton (b. 1887). That same year, Joseph signed his World War I registration, listing his wife as next of kin and his occupation as merchant. He was not drafted. The couple had one child, Elva Mildred Kibler (February 15, 1920–September 24, 2005). Following the war, in 1919, Joseph Kibler raised his store and set it on logs. Using a team of mules, and lots of help from family and neighbors, he rolled the store down Coleman's Road to Concord Road. He then turned east and rolled it another four hundred yards to his

Salem Methodist-Episcopal Church in Draperville (later Kiblerville) was dedicated on June 24, 1893. This 1908 postcard could be of Reverend Kibler, with horse and buggy. *Courtesy of William C. Gregory.*

brother's blacksmith shop. There he established "Kibler's Store." Then, he built a home next to the store on a parcel of land that he purchased from Manton on February 16, 1921 (after the home was built).

The community became known as "Kiblerville" in 1920. Next door to Joseph and Mary Kibler were Manton and Elizabeth (b. 1897), with their two children. Living with Joseph and Mary was another brother, John Lee Kibler, who was serving a trial as a Methodist minister with the Salem M.E. Church, which was located next door to the home. He was residing there with his wife and four-month-old son.

Also living with Joseph was Mary's widowed mother, Luvan, age sixty-eight, whom they were taking care of. Soon after the 1920 census, John Lee Kibler and family moved to the Bluestone District of Mecklenburg County, their first church. In 1922, Joe's youngest brother, James A., moved into the home with his new bride, Lula. Lula had recently graduated from college and accepted a teaching position with a local county school, located at the Concord Baptist Church. Lula became the piano player for the Salem M.E. Church.

Shortly after their arrival, James purchased a small parcel from his brother Manton and built a garage next to the church. He was advertising in the

Kibler's Store is still in the community but is currently in operation as an upholstery shop, owned by Alfred Card. *Photo by Betty McKinney Caknipe.*

Chase City News Progress on April 23, 1923: "James Kibler's Garage on the new South Hill Road. Auto repairing by men that know how—parts and accessories—blacksmithing and wheelwright. First class work guaranteed." Ads also appeared in the 1924 County Business Directory: "wagon repair—horseshoeing in Kiblerville." Next to these were ads for "J.A. Kibler's Store 7 miles east of Chase City with general merchandise, dry goods, shoes, notions, confectionary, cold drinks, smokes, tobaccos—buy and sell country produce—filling station, auto accessories, gas and oil."

Also in 1923, Lula Kibler began to produce and direct plays in and by the local community. The plays were performed at the Concord Baptist Church (established in 1817 as a Methodist Church, but changed to Baptist by 1855), as it had a much larger seating capacity than did the Salem church. The plays were well attended, and the community could purchase tickets from Kibler's Store or from Walton's Store in nearby Scotts Crossroads. On March 21, 1924, the performance was so well received that an encore performance sold out for the following weekend. The play was *A Poor Married Man*, directed by Mrs. J.A. Kibler. A 1924 newspaper social column stated, "Joe Kibler's wife, and daughter Elva, are spending a month visiting relatives in Baltimore."

In 1925, the social column included a section titled "Kiblerville," and it seems Mrs. Kibler and Elva went to Baltimore each year for several years. In 1925, James Kibler had completed building their home. With the lack of work for wagons and wagon repairs, Manton joined James in the auto repair business. In 1927, business was doing well, so they purchased some parcels of land and Joe turned the business over to Manton. Joe went to work for Jeffreys' Motor Company in Chase City in 1929 as a new car salesman. Manton sold the business during the Depression and moved his family to Richmond, Henrico County, Virginia. Schools consolidated in 1932, and the country schools moved to a central location in Chase City.

James continued to sell automobiles through the Depression. He was selected to serve on the board of directors of the South Central Fair Association, Inc., and in 1948, he was hired as general manager of the fair. Joe continued to operate the store throughout the Depression, and it became a much-needed force of stability for the community. He provided a place for comradeship for the local farmers and families during those trying days and those that followed during World War II and the Korean Conflict. In 1954, he began receiving social security at the age of seventy-two. He continued to operate the store into the 1960s, before he died in 1966.

Miss Elva, as everyone knew her, was first a schoolteacher and then, when schools consolidated in 1955, she became the Bluestone High School counselor, the position from which she retired. She lived her entire life in the family home, never married and had no children. She died in 2005, the last Kibler of Kiblerville.

EDUCATION IN SOUTHSIDE: ONE EARLY SUCCESS STORY

CHASE CITY HIGH SCHOOL

The first successful school in Southside was the Ebenezer Academy, circa 1784, in Brunswick County. It was taken over in 1792 by the Methodist Church, around 1804 by the Presbyterians and around 1840 by the county as a public school called the Brunswick Academy. It closed during the Civil War. Warrenton Male Academy in Warren County, North Carolina, began operation in 1788 and served as a feeder school for Randolph Macon College after it opened in 1832. Many schools and academies were begun, with most being one-room schoolhouses (field schools), or occasionally two-room houses. Most, however, were privately owned, located in someone's home or a local church, or sometimes a family would hire a tutor to live in their home and teach the children. Successful schools were academies, mostly for boys, which included the community, county government and local church(s) involvement in their operation. If one of these components was missing, the life of the school was short-lived. Compulsory education funded by the government didn't really take hold in the United States until after 1931. One of the most successful early schools in Southside that included these elements was the Chase City High School, which began as partly public funded, with town and county support, along with tuition.

Through the efforts of the Chase City District School Board, the Mecklenburg County Board of Supervisors and local, concerned citizens, funding was secured and plans were approved for Chase City Agricultural Consolidated High School in 1907—the first of its kind in the area. Although the building was not completed, the school began in 1908 but without water, sewer, electricity or excavation of the grounds and sidewalks. Students were brought to school by buggy, on foot or on horseback, which was difficult to manage without pasture and stables available. Many families from the outlying areas had family and friends who lived in town, and arrangements were made for some students to live in Chase City on Tuesday through Thursday nights and return home on weekends.

The Town of Chase City decided to capitalize on the concept. Anyone boarding a student had to secure a boardinghouse license. The license cost was determined by the number of boarders. Thus, the family and friends were now guesthouse operators, with costs being passed on to the students' families. Work continued while school was in session and into the following summer. With a dedication ceremony the week following Labor Day in 1909, the school was officially opened. This was primarily a day of celebration, and the festivities ended with a "chicken chase" contest by the students. The prize was that if you caught a chicken, you could take it home for supper or whatever.

When the school officially opened, there were only two teachers: Samuel Page Duke and his wife, Lucile Duke. Samuel Duke, who had a bachelor's degree, was born in September 1885, the son of Reverend Thomas P. Duke (b. June 1833) and Virginia G. Duke (b. August 1840), who were residing in Danville, Virginia, in 1880 and Chatham, Virginia, in 1900. Samuel had three sisters and two brothers. There was another child in the home, along with her mother. Lucile Duke was born in Texas around 1889 and came to Virginia, apparently for her education, for she received her Bachelor of Science degree. In 1908, when the family arrived in Chase City, they rented a home on the south side of Sycamore Street (formerly Abbeyville Road) at the intersection of Endly Street. It was only a short one-hundred-yard walk to the high school and next door to town druggist, Peter Maddox. The 1910 graduating class consisted of ten students.

In the fall of 1910, Duke appeared before town council at numerous monthly meetings. He was persistent with securing sidewalks from Main Street to the high school and crosswalks at the school across Second Street (the streets were graded dirt, and when it rained, they became a muddy quagmire). Duke and the school board met with several local farmers in

The 1908 Chase City High School still serves the community. Today, it is Maple Manor Apartments for seniors and low-income residents. *Photo by author.*

1909. The school board offered to hire the farmers to establish a route where they could come, pick up the children in their wagon, bring them to school in the morning and take them home in the afternoon. This met with great success—so much so that in the 1920s and 1930s, before school buses, farmers would purchase pickup trucks as their personal vehicle especially to transport the students. In all these situations, weather was always a factor, and thus, school buses were a welcomed creation.

In 1911, Duke began to focus on abolishing the license for families taking in student boarders, as there were three high schools in Chase City: Chase City High School, Southside Female Academy and Thyne Institute in Fairview (on the north edge of town). It appears that Duke aligned with the Virginia State Normal School Board. In 1911, he was still attending council meetings but to encourage an exemption for teachers and students who would be flocking to Chase City if he could convince the State of Virginia Board of Education to hold its summer conference in town. He wanted the town to host a Chase City Institute for Teachers in 1910, with classes to be held primarily at Southside Female Institute.

The conference would also include a state teachers college training program to certify new teachers. (On a note about teacher certification, my great-aunt Elizabeth [Lee] Ward told me that she graduated from school in Scottsburg, Halifax County, Virginia. She went to a normal school, secured a teaching certification and began teaching, which she did for three years. In 1920, she met the love of her life, and they were married and soon had a child. She retired from teaching. The following month, after the birth of her first child, she turned the ripe old age of eighteen.) Teacher training was a six-week program, and an education, for most students, included only up to the sixth grade, although in 1930, education became mandatory. Children were, for the first time, required to attend school. The school program included high school, which included grades seven through eleven. Also, children were no longer charged tuition for attending school.

Duke did secure the annual conference and the normal school. The town council waived boardinghouse license fees for the conference and then extended it for all school students through the fall regular school term and into the following year. It appears the conference was a success, as the Little Mecklenburg Hotel, Barnett Hotel, Jackson Boarding House, Gregory Hotel and Southside Academy dormitory were all filled. The Wootton Boarding House, which had just opened on South Main Street, was also filled. It was clearly a success for the career of Duke. Within a couple years, Duke and his family left Chase City. It appears that the conference came to Chase City with an ulterior motive: to consider the area for a normal college.

Following Duke's departure from Chase City, the family relocated to Harrisonburg, Virginia. There, he accepted the position of president of the new Virginia Normal School, which began in 1915. He was still there in 1940, with Lucile, Robert (now twenty-two) and Marshall (twenty), but the school was now a college and was renamed Madison College. Subsequently, it was renamed James Madison University for James Madison Duke, son of Samuel and Lucile.

The Chase City High School, the new Thyne High School (previously grades one through six) and Southside Academy (having been recently taken over by the Virginia Baptist Association) were all accredited by the Commonwealth of Virginia in 1910. Then in the week following Labor Day in 1917, a new Chase City Elementary School was dedicated, offering grades one through six, and a ribbon cutting was held for a new athletic field.

In 1919, behind the high school, a new building that housed the agricultural/vocational school downstairs and home economics school upstairs was dedicated. In 1946, following World War II, the vocational building was

In this CCHS football team photo from 1942, none of the players has been identified. This is the athletic field of 1909, with the elementary school of 1917 at right and the vocational/home economics building behind the team. *Courtesy of Mark Colgate.*

also used as an agricultural studies center for returning veterans. It became a Veterans Administration–approved trade school, and next door, a new building was constructed for a Chase City Cannery to teach high school students and adults from the community the science of preserving foods.

Following the opening of the Chase City High School, new modern schools were being opened throughout the county within five years. In Clarksville, a new high school opened (torn down in 1970 for a strip mall), as well as Lacrosse (burned in 1942, rebuilt as an elementary school) and South Hill (burned in 1952). Boydton built a graded school, consisting of grades one through eleven but no high school. All the schools were consolidated in 1955. Chase City High School is the only one of the school buildings still standing.

In 1982, Mary Alice and Billy Park purchased the school complex and converted the vocational building to a restaurant called the Angus Inn. In 1992, their two sons, William and Richard, began acquiring schools for historical preservation and to develop affordable, multi-family dwellings, focusing on seniors, the disabled or both. They formed Pinnacle Construction and Development Corporation of Charlottesville, Virginia, and purchased the Chase City High School complex. After investing over $1.33 million in renovations to bring the buildings up to code while still protecting the historical integrity, Maple Manor Apartments opened for occupancy. It has received numerous awards, including the Governor's Housing Achievement Award and many federal awards.

On September 9, 2009, in celebration of the one-hundred-year anniversary, the cornerstone from the high school was removed, exposing a time capsule, which had been placed there on November 13, 1908. The contents, examined by this author (thanks to the Parks family), included a November 13, 1908 copy of the *Progress*; a Bible; a copy of the July 31, 1907 *Mecklenburg County School Report and Budget*; a flyer for the November 24–27, 1907 state teachers conference; a 1908 *Volume of the State of Virginia School Laws*; a copy of the July 31, 1907 *Chase City School District Annual Report*; and a volume of the *State of Virginia Annual School Report* for 1905–6 and 1906–7 (bound by string). There was also a handwritten list of the names of two teachers, a secretary and 130 students (water damaged) and a handwritten list of the building committee members, which included W.A. Broocks as chairman, as well as A. Leach and J.J. Mason (all members of the Chase City School Board). In addition, there were associate members listed, including F.B. Reamy, T.E. Roberts and James Hardy.

....

The Piedmont Region claims several major historical accomplishments for the commonwealth and the nation. As the "Old Race Horse Region" and the "Cradle of Methodism" in the eastern United States, hosting one of the first Methodist academies and the first successful continuous Methodist college in the United States, Randolph Macon College (1830) in Boydton, Virginia, the area was primed to provide great leaders in history. But the underscore of the area is the people who used adventure, initiative and ambition, coupled with a traditional southern gentile demeanor and charm, Old and New World religion and a learned society, to continue to evolve. One acquaintance of this author from Colorado, who is a computer whiz for the Silicon Valley, told me recently that the buzz in his circle is that this region and continuing south to Charlotte, North Carolina, is to become the East Coast Silicon Valley of the future. But for those of us fortunate enough to be born and raised here, it's just home.

ABOUT THE AUTHOR

J ohn Caknipe is a native of Southside Virginia, with family members having participated in every military conflict since the Revolutionary War and himself in Vietnam. As a former Special Forces noncommissioned officer in the U.S. Army and a disabled veteran, his career has spanned nearly four decades of teaching and two decades of counseling services. He has researched and written about the evolution of the Piedmont area since 2007, including three volumes of the Images of America series, the "Unsung Heroes" series of stories for the *News Progress* and the "Remember the Gray" series for the *South Hill Enterprise*. His work was selected by the Library of Virginia for inclusion in a volume of the Virginia Biography series.

His work has also appeared in the credits of Ark Media for the PBS TV show *Finding Your Roots* and in the NBC TV show *Who Do You Think You Are?* Having completed graduate degrees from Siena Heights College, Eastern Michigan University and International Graduate School, he has served as a college professor of psychology for over thirty years, currently with Southside Virginia Community College in South Boston, Virginia. He and his wife reside in Clarksville.

Visit us at
www.historypress.net

....

This title is also available as an e-book